Finches
FOR
DUMMIES®

by Nikki Moustaki

WILEY

Wiley Publishing, Inc.

Finches For Dummies®

Published by
Wiley Publishing, Inc.
111 River St.
Hoboken, NJ 07030-5774
www.wiley.com

Copyright © 2007 by Wiley Publishing, Inc., Indianapolis, Indiana

Published by Wiley Publishing, Inc., Indianapolis, Indiana

Published simultaneously in Canada

For general information on our other products and services or to obtain technical support, please contact our Customer Care Department within the U.S. at 800-762-2974, outside the U.S. at 317-572-3993, or fax 317-572-4002.

Wiley also publishes its books in a variety of electronic formats. Some content that appears in print may not be available in electronic books.

Library of Congress Control Number: available from publisher

ISBN: 978-0-470-12161-0

Manufactured in the United States of America

10 9 8 7 6 5 4 3 2 1

1B/RV/QT/QX/IN

Publisher's Acknowledgments

Project Editor: Elizabeth Kuball
Acquisitions Editor: Stacy Kennedy
Technical Editor: Becky Margison
Composition Services: Indianapolis Composition Services Department
Cover Photo: © Jorg & Petra Wegner/Animals Animals
Cartoon: Rich Tennant, www.the5thwave.com

About the Author

Nikki Moustaki, M.A., M.F.A., is an Avian Care and Behavior Consultant and the author of several books on birds and bird behavior. She has kept and/or bred lovebirds, cockatiels, budgies (parakeets), lories, macaws, amazons, conures, finches, canaries, ringnecks, and brotergeris. She advocates responsible bird care and encourages everyone to participate in rescue efforts.

Table of Contents

The 5th Wave

By Rich Tennant

"If your finch is going to sing the soprano part, at least keep him in tempo."

Chapter 1

Finches: More Than Just Pretty, Chatty Birds

In This Chapter

▶ Knowing what a finch is

▶ Understanding how a finch is put together

▶ Looking at the different varieties of finches

▶ Getting in touch with finch clubs and societies

*F*inches are charming companions, adding a little bit of life to an empty corner of any home. Whether you plan on having just a pair, or would like a whole aviary full, finches offer a glimpse into the natural world, and give keepers hours of watching pleasure. They are easy to care for, are relatively quiet, and some are prettier than a rainbow. What more could you ask for?

First Things First: Using This Book

Finches For Dummies is a book I wrote for people interested in finches — whether you're a parent buying this book for yourself or your child or you're a kid buying it for yourself using your hard-earned cash. Maybe you just bought a finch and need the essential scoop on getting set up as well as general care information. Or, you may already have a finch and you need a refresher on the best way to take care of your pet or want to understand it better. Perhaps you're ready for a new pet but aren't sure if a finch is right for you and yours. If any of the above describes you, keep on readin'.

This book is a reference, so you don't have to read it in order from start to finish. Begin with Chapter 4 if you need basic setup information, flip to Chapter 6 if you're thinking about breeding finches, or head to Chapter 2 if you're still on the fence about adding a finch to your family. (Although those of you who prefer to start at the beginning and read until you reach the back cover are welcome to do so. I'll never tell.)

As you read, keep an eye out for text in *italics,* which indicates a new term and a nearby definition — no need to spend time hunting through a glossary. And `monofont` points out Web addresses for additional information worth checking out. You'll also run into a few sidebars (the occasional gray box); although the information in the sidebars is good, it's not essential to the discussion at hand, so skip 'em if you want to.

While reading *Finches For Dummies,* be on the lookout for these icons, sprinkled here and there:

This icon flags tips and tricks that will help you be the best finch friend you can be.

This icons points out information that's so important you'll want to be sure to remember it.

This icon highlights information on things that could harm you or your finch.

This icon flags information that you can use to impress your friends with your amazing bird knowledge, but it isn't absolutely necessary, so don't feel the need to memorize it.

What Is a Finch?

The term *finch* is actually a very broad term, encompassing hundreds of species and subspecies, from canaries to sparrows. In general, finches are small song birds that come in an amazing variety of colors, shapes, and sizes. They all have short, cone-shaped bills adapted to the type of food they typically eat. All finches are seed eaters, but most will eat other vegetation and insects as well.

Finches have been kept as companions for hundreds of years. The Chinese and Japanese have been breeding finches since the 1600s — for example, the society finch (also known as the Bengalese finch) is not found in the wild because it was developed by humans, much as breeds of dogs were. It is also one of the most widely kept finches today. The canary is the oldest domesticated bird, having been bred in captivity for many centuries, and, like dogs, bred for certain traits (its ancestor, the serin finch, is still found in the wild in the Canary Islands). Finches that have a long history with humans do very well as companion birds. They tend to be hardier and less skittish than other types of birds, who haven't been around the bird scene for as long.

In the following sections, I show you what makes a finch a finch.

Where finches come from

Because they comprise such a large group, finches are found in every corner of the world. Even the Galapagos Islands are home to 13 species of finches, all of which were studied by famed British naturalist, Charles Darwin. The finch was one of the animals used in Darwin's Theory of Evolution.

You can only keep finches that aren't native to North America — this goes for all birds, actually. If a bird is native to North America, housing it is illegal. Birds that fall into this category include the American goldfinch, the cardinal, and the pine siskin, among others.

Most of the companion finches available for purchase are native to other countries but were bred in captivity where you live.

The many species of finches

One of the more fascinating things about finches is their seeming endless variety. They range from very delicate to very hardy birds, in all colors of the rainbow. Some are drab and others are exceptionally vivid. Many species are *dimorphic,* which means that you can distinguish the gender of the bird just by looking at it. Others are *monomorphic,* which means that you can't visually distinguish the genders of the birds.

All finches are scientifically grouped under the order *Passeriformes.* Passerines (which is what *Passeriformes* are called) comprise more than half of the bird species in the world, with nearly 5,400 members. Not all Passerines are finches, but all finches are Passerines.

Though no one expects you to become an *ornithologist* (someone who studies birds), in order to provide a good home for your companion finch it can be helpful to understand where your bird is classified in the scheme of things. Here are the four different groups of finches:

✔ **Fringillidae:** The 138 members of this group are often called the "true" finches. This family includes the canaries, chaffinches, some siskins, rosefinches, goldfinches, and bullfinches. These finches are adapted to crush seeds and, as a result, they have strong skulls and jaws. These finches are found on all continents.

✔ **Passeridae:** This group of 38 finches includes sparrows and snowfinches. Formerly found only in Europe and the surrounding areas, these finches have now been introduced to habitats all over the world. Two types of Passeridae are commonly found in the United States, including the house sparrow. As a group, they are hardy and gregarious songbirds.

✔ **Estrildidae:** Included in this group of 139 birds are some the most popular companion finches, including grass finches, parrot finches, waxbills, society finches, greenfinches, serins, firefinches, firetails, quailfinches, gouldian finches, mannikins, nuns, munias, java sparrows, cordon bleus, cut throats, and zebra finches. The majority of finches in this group are from a temperate climate, preferring warm weather. They tend to be flocking birds and are all seed-eaters.

✔ **Ploceidae:** This group has 117 members, including the whydahs (also called widowbirds) and weavers (also called bishops). They are found primarily in Africa and India and can be more aggressive in their response to other birds than some of the more commonly kept species.

One of the longest domesticated and most popular varieties of finch is the well-known canary (see Figure 1-1). Canaries come in a variety of colors, from bright yellow, like the famous Tweety Bird, to brown, gray, white, and *variegated* (having either regular or uneven dark markings). Canaries are delicate birds, originally from the Canary Islands, and have been a popular pet in Europe since the 16th century, perhaps even earlier.

Most people buy a canary for his beautiful song. The males are the singers of the species, and they're generally the gender that you'll want to keep if you want to hear singing in your home. The females can make great companions too, but they won't launch into song the way a male will.

The canary's song depends largely on the type of canary that you choose. Some canaries sing a variety of songs, while others are trained only to sing in a certain manner — yes, canaries have to be trained to sing. Many breeders keep an "expert" singer, a canary with a particularly masterful song, in a cage along side of his young males. The youngsters will learn from this maestro and, hopefully, pick up the essentials of beautiful singing. Don't worry if you don't have a master singer to teach the young males their trade — CDs and tapes of canary song work just as well (you can buy these at some pet stores).

Figure 1-1: Canaries are among the most popular types of finch.

Size differences

Finches can vary in size from about 3 inches in length to about 8 inches in length. Some finches are very tiny, such as the gold-breasted waxbill, measuring in at under 3 inches. The whydah, who is only 5 inches in length, has a tail that can reach 15 inches during breeding season.

Temperament differences

In terms of companion quality, most finches are the same. Some are more skittish than others, but for the most part, they all make wonderful companions. Some can be more demanding in terms of nutritional needs or housing, and others are far easier, such as the zebra, society, or owl finch.

Finches aren't aggressive toward children or other pets. The reverse is far more likely to be true. However, some species of finches are aggressive toward other species of finches, and all varieties of finches will have more of a tendency toward aggression during the breeding season.

I see your true colors shining through . . .

Some canaries, like the red factor canary, will turn various shades of red and orange if they're fed certain foods, such as paprika. Although this practice is forbidden in most show circles, it is actively practiced by many companion owners.

Don't try to feed your other types of canaries the color food — only the red factor has the genetic predisposition to show what it eats though its feathers.

If you're going to keep a large *aviary* (a home for birds that's large enough for an adult human to walk into), and you wish to have more than one species represented, do some research ahead of time to find out which species will be most likely to get along. For example, weavers are quite aggressive and the males will hurt, or even kill, other species and other males of their own species. Society finches, on the other hand, get along so well that more than a dozen of them will try to crunch themselves into one nest to sleep for the night.

Most of the time, finches will shy away from human contact. Taming a finch to appreciate human contact is sometimes possible, but that depends a great deal upon the individual finch and will usually require more patience and effort than most bird guardians are willing to devote. Remember that your companion finch is a very delicate creature and easily frightened. Too sudden a shock or fright can be fatal to your little friend.

The finch lifespan

Most finches live to be between five and ten years old, with some variations among species. Some have been reported living 15 years or more. Although it's very rare, finch guardians have also reported that their finches have lived up to 27 years! Now that's a well-cared-for finch!

Anatomy of a Finch

Knowing the parts of your finch is a good idea, so that you can describe a problem to the veterinarian if you have to do so. Knowing the different parts of your finch is also a good idea if you're going to breed or show your birds. This way you can speak like an expert with other hobbyists. Here are the parts of your finch you'll want to be familiar with (see Figure 1-2 for an illustration).

Crown: The *crown* is simply the top of the head. It's an important word to know in finch-speak because many finches are identified by the color of the crown.

Nares: The *nares* (nostrils) are at the top of the beak and may not be visible because they're often covered by fine feathers.

Beak: The upper and lower mandibles make up the finch's beak. In the case of a finch, it's short, wide, and rather triangular in shape. This is for crushing the tiny hard seeds that make up most of your finch's diet. The beak is made from the same tough material that makes your fingernails.

Ear and ear coverts: Your finch has tiny flat holes for ears, and they're covered by *coverts,* or tiny flaps of skin bearing feathers, which protect them from the wind when flying. This is why your finch's ears are difficult to see.

Eyes: The finch's eyes are on either side of his head so that it can see a wider area than you can see with your forward-facing eyes. A finch needs a wider range of vision because it's a prey animal and needs to be on the alert for predators. Finches, like many birds, have a third eyelid called a *nictitating membrane,* a thin semitransparent lid that washes the eye like a squeegee and closes for protection.

Throat: The throat is just beneath the beak and extends to the breast. Many finch species are identified partially by the color of the plumage at the throat.

Nape: The nape is the back of the neck.

Shoulder: The shoulder is at the top of the wing, nearest the finch's back.

Breast: The breast is just below the throat.

Foot: Everything that most people think of as a bird's leg is actually a bird's foot. That's why the "knee" appears to bend the wrong way — what you may be thinking of as the knee is actually the bird's heel. As for toes, finches have three front toes and one that grips to the rear.

Vent: The vent is where your finch eliminates. In a human, this would be a combined anus and urethra. Birds do not urinate.

Primary feathers: Finches have ten long primary wing feathers that aid in flight.

Secondary feathers: The secondary feathers on the wing occur after the primary feathers; they're smaller and closer to the body than the primaries are.

Rump: The rump is beneath the primary flight feathers on the finch's lower back.

Mantle: The *mantle* is the bird's back.

Crop: The *crop* is a sac-like organ that's kind of like a "first stomach." It's where the food goes immediately after being swallowed and is located at the breast.

Gizzard: The *gizzard* is like a "second stomach" that grinds food to digest it.

Syrinx: The syrinx is equivalent to vocal chords in humans. It allows finches to sing when air is pushed through it.

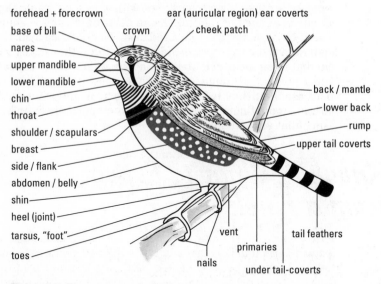

Figure 1-2: The anatomy of a finch.

Chapter 2

Is a Finch Your Perfect Pet?

In This Chapter

▶ Knowing what to expect from your finch

▶ Understanding how your other pets can harm your finch

▶ Figuring out what to do with your finch when you leave on vacation

▶ Knowing what to ask yourself before you buy a finch

*I*f you're trying to decide whether to bring a finch into your home, you've come to the right chapter. But don't worry — even if you already have a finch, this chapter has something for you. Here you'll figure out what to expect from a finch (from its seemingly endless energy to the messes it makes) and what your finch expects from you. I walk you through the challenges posed by children and other pets (whether they're birds or not). I also give you information on keeping more than one finch and fill you in on breeding finches (and what you should consider before you do it).

Knowing What to Expect from a Finch

Finches have the reputation of being a small bird that you place in a small cage, much like a goldfish on display in a bowl. Many people believe that one of these smaller birds will live for only two to three years at the most and that there is little point in becoming deeply attached to a finch because the bird won't live very long. Nothing could be farther from the truth!

A finch makes a wonderful companion, and if you take good care of him, you'll be able to enjoy your finch for between 3 and 10 years, perhaps even more. Most finches are curious, amazingly intelligent, and develop very distinctive personalities. You won't want to miss out on the very real pleasure of getting to know and love them.

In the following sections, I fill you in on some of the traits you should expect from a finch, so you know what to expect.

Activity

Finches are very busy and active little birds. They spend a great deal of their day flying from perch to perch and interacting with their companions. They play with simple toys, usually preferring something shiny. They also build nests, both for sleeping and for breeding. Finches are much simpler than parrots, which need a lot of out-of-the-cage time. Some people do allow their companion finches to fly around their home, but this isn't the norm.

Taming a finch: Not for the impatient

If you have the time, you may want to undertake the difficult and delicate task of attempting to tame your finch. There is no joy quite like having your tiny feathered friend perch on your shoulder and snuggle trustingly up to your neck, but be aware that coaxing a finch to this degree of trust takes a tremendous amount of time and patience, and most finches will simply never accept a close human bond.

If you're still determined to finger-tame your finch, you definitely want a bird who has been bred and raised in captivity. You'll also want to adopt or purchase a bird that is just old enough to leave the nest. First, get the bird comfortable with your presence. Talk to her soothingly and move slowly near the cage. Offer millet spray through the cage bars and talk to her as she eats it. Develop a noise that's all your own, such as a distinctive whistle or clicking or kissing sound, and do it every time you enter the house and/or approach the cage. All these things will start making the bird more comfortable with your presence.

After she's comfortable with you, open the door to the cage (only if the cage is in a safe, bird-proofed room — do not move the cage to a new location or you're going to have to start over). Allow the finch to come out on her own. Sit still, make your distinctive noise, and hold some millet spray. If you've succeeded in gaining her trust, she may come to you for a treat. Don't push it! If she doesn't come out the first time, just keep trying each day until she does. It may happen that the bird will never come to you. It's all up to her — you can't force contact.

When you want her to return to her cage, put something in it that she absolutely loves, like egg food. If she doesn't return, you may have to use a bird net to gently capture her and put her back. Or wait until dusk or turn out the lights in the room and she may go back on her own, but this isn't always the case. If not, look for where she has gone to *roost* (sleep) and gently grasp her and put her back in the cage.

Noise

Finches do sing, although they aren't nearly as noisy as the more raucous and larger species of birds, especially parrots. Most people greatly enjoy finches' soft twittering, cheeps, and peeps. Usually, the male finch is the one who sings — and nearly always to his mate or potential mate. The more finches you have, the louder they will be, though the noise from even a flock of finches rarely annoys their guardian or the neighbors.

 A charming revelation about finches has recently come out of the scientific community (though they probably didn't mean it to be charming): Finches dream about singing. Studies on zebra finches have shown that they're so devoted to learning their song that they even dream about it.

Enjoyment

You can look forward to many hours of enjoyment watching your finches go about their daily lives. If you pay attention to what they're doing, you'll probably find that they provide more entertainment than television!

Finches aren't considered hands-on companions, though some people do manage to tame their finches or hand-feed babies so that they're tame. These tame finches are few and far between, but they're not a myth — "taming" is generally done out of necessity, because a baby has been abandoned or fallen from the nest.

Mess

Your finch will always require a good deal of housecleaning. Finches scatter loose feathers, bird seed, and water, along with anything else they are in regular contact with, which is why their cages should be located above a floor that you can clean easily.

If they fly free for occasional periods, you'll have to clean some droppings from furnishings and carpets also. Chances are that you won't object seriously to this if you're enchanted by birds, but your roommates and guests may suggest "training" your bird to teach him less messy behavior. Keeping a bird from being messy is completely impossible, of course, so if you're around someone who seriously objects to ongoing mess, you may want to consider a different type of animal companion.

Knowing What Your Finch Expects from You

Your finch — unlike your family, friends, coworkers, and just about everybody else you come into contact with — won't expect much from you. But he will need proper care and attention so that he can live a happy and healthy life — and you need to know what your finch requires in order to help him do exactly that.

Proper care for finches consists of more than just putting seed and water in a cage. Your finch relies on you for all his needs: proper housing, nutrition, and safety. You're responsible for every aspect of his life. In the following sections, I let you know what your parakeet needs from you, but here's a list of basics to get you started:

- **A clean cage:** You need to clean your finch's cage every day. Once a week, you need to clean the cage and the surrounding area more thoroughly.

- **Water:** You need to offer your finch fresh water twice a day. Throw out the water from the day before (or the hours before) and replace it so that your finch always has a fresh water supply.

- **Food:** Offer and change fresh foods once a day — and not just seeds. Finches need a considerable quantity of fresh vegetables, greens, live food, and egg food, in addition to bird seed. Just as with water, if your finch hasn't eaten all the food you gave him the day before, throw out the old food and replace it with new. (*Note:* You should change the water twice a day, but you only need to add or change the food once a day.)

- **Attention to his health:** Your finch can't just fly out to the vet's office when he feels a little under the weather. You need to watch your bird closely for signs of illness, and take him to the veterinarian if you suspect something is wrong or if your bird has an accident of some sort.

- **A safe home:** When you bring a finch into your home, you need to make sure it's a safe place for your bird to live. (See Chapter 4 for more information on finch-proofing your home.) Also make sure that your finch's cage is away from drafts and that the room where he lives doesn't get too cold or too warm.

In addition to these basics of bird care, your finch needs other things from you, covered in the following sections.

Vacationing without your finches

A well-behaved dog or a cat can often be left with an automatic feeder, toilet facilities of some kind, and plenty of water for periods of up to a couple of days, but finches are tiny creatures with a very fast metabolism. Your finches could literally die of hunger or thirst in the course of a single day, so you'll need to make careful and reliable arrangements to care for your birds if you're away from home for more than a day.

Though you can travel with your finch, travel can be difficult and disorienting for finches. In addition, these small birds are extremely susceptible to illness when stressed, so exposure to drafts or cold can literally be fatal. Try to leave your bird home with a reliable bird-sitter if possible.

A good home

A good home for finches provides them with absolutely everything they need to be healthy and long-lived:

- ✔ **They need as large a cage as your wallet and space can afford.**

- ✔ **They need access to direct sunlight or to be provided with bird-specific full-spectrum lighting.** If the cage is in direct sunlight, the finches should have a shady, cooler place where they can retreat.

- ✔ **They need to live in moderate temperatures, ideally somewhere between 70° and 80° F (21° to 26° C).** Some finches that aren't from the tropics can handle winter weather if they're acclimated to it — be sure to allow them to adjust gradually to the falling temperatures.

- ✔ **Finches also need cleanliness.** You need to clean your finch's cage frequently. Bird waste is fairly inoffensive and easily cleaned when it's relatively fresh, but it dries every bit as hard as concrete in a very short time, and then powders to a fine dust that is dangerous for humans (and finches) to breathe for extended periods.

The longer you wait to clean your finch's cage, the more time you'll need to spend cleaning it. Most bird-care experts recommend cleaning a cage at least once a week, but giving it a quick once-over daily is easier and far less trouble.

Cages and accessories for birds can be surprisingly expensive, and a proper diet for your finches is an ongoing expense that you should also consider. In addition, unless you're very fortunate, you may have unplanned veterinary expenses from time to time, as well as the frequent, necessary, and planned veterinary examinations to keep your birds happy and healthy.

Routine

In the wild, finches schedule their days around the sun. They understand the seasons and how to behave when water or food is scarce or plentiful. In nature, the same events happen day after day, year after year, and these birds are programmed to go with the flow.

Your finch is pretty much the same bird with the same programming, but his life is far different. Even if his life is cushy, the lack of routine can become stressful. Finches are genetically programmed to do certain things at certain times of the day — for example, they want to eat in the morning, when they're hungriest. You can snack all night if you want, but finches have an innate understanding that if they're snacking at midnight and making noise, they're fair game for a lurking predator.

Create a routine and try to stick with it. Your finch should know exactly when you're going to feed him, when you're going to clean his cage, and when it's time for bed. If you keep a routine with your finch, he may eventually alert *you* when you've missed a step. If your life is hectic, just do the best you can.

Deciding Whether a Finch Is Right for You

Adopting or purchasing any animal companion is a serious responsibility. By keeping any creature in captivity, you become responsible for its health and happiness for the duration of its natural lifespan. In the case of finches, that lifespan could be fairly short, so making every day a good one for these little birds is important.

Ask yourself, before you consider bringing a finch into your home, whether your lifestyle is one that can provide a happy life and home for your companion birds. Also, think about whether you can commit to whatever changes will be necessary to provide a good environment for your new friends for as long as they live.

In the following sections, I offer some questions to ask yourself before you consider keeping a finch.

Is your family in agreement?

You'll need to make certain that the other people who share your house and your life also share your enthusiasm for your little feathered pals. Have a family meeting and discuss your plans to have and/or breed finches. Though finches are much less trouble than many other types of birds, you and your housemates will have to put up with a certain amount of mess and noise — and a complaining or unhappy family member can take a lot of the joy out of the experience of keeping finches.

Though some finches can be tamed enough to accept human handling, taming a finch takes a very long time and a great deal of work. The vast majority of finches, even those bred in captivity, are going to be frightened if someone tries to touch them. Touching an untamed finch is unkind, and if the behavior is prolonged or rough, it can be terrifying and even deadly. Everyone in the house should understand this and put the finches' needs above his or her own.

Do you have any smokers in the house?

Tobacco smoking absolutely must not be permitted near your finch. Finches have very delicate respiratory systems, and tobacco smoke is deadly to them. Everyone in the house must also know not to spray any household cleansers or air fresheners, or light candles near the bird — for the same reason.

Houseguests

You have to ask all your houseguests — whether they're just visiting for an afternoon or staying for a month — to respect your finch and her housing. If the person doesn't know much about birds, and if his only bird contact has been with a parakeet or another hands-on bird, he may not understand why your finch won't come out to perch on his finger. Be sure to explain that finches are different from other birds.

If you're having a party, you can always post a note on your finch's housing, or simply move her from the room. If you think your party may become especially rowdy, be sure to move your finch to a room that's off-limits to the partygoers.

Be sure that, before you bring a finch into the home, everyone you live with is okay with these restrictions. You want to get their agreement *before* you keep a finch — otherwise, you're not being fair to your future feathered friend.

Is your home also home to children?

Very young children or unruly older children can be a danger to your finches. Inappropriate handling, feeding of unhealthy items, and excessive noise can stress a finch — or even kill him. Children should be taught not to handle the cage or the finches, not to put anything into the cage, and to use "indoor voices" around the birds.

Do you have other pets?

Dogs and cats definitely consider finches to be tasty snacks, as you can see in Figure 2-1. Even other birds pose a threat — a cross-species friendship is rare, and a finch doesn't have any defenses against a more powerful bird. Even a very frightened or aggressive finch is unlikely to have a painful bite — except to another finch.

Figure 2-1: Never allow other pets to have contact with your finches.

Giving finches as gifts

Giving an adorable bird as a gift is often tempting, and finches may seem perfect at such a time. However, the commitment and responsibility involved in making a home for a finch is pretty big, and the decision to make this commitment is not one that should be made by another person. Unless you're absolutely sure that the person wants and is ready to care for the finches, give a gift certificate to the pet shop instead.

If you have other animals, your finch's cage should be inaccessible to them, and your finch should never be allowed to fly free when the other animals are loose. Also, standing water, such as that in a fish tank, toilet bowl, or deep dog dish can pose a drowning threat to your finches.

One, Two — or More: Increasing Your Finch Population

Some finches are social birds, and they need interaction with other finches to be happy and well-adjusted. Consider purchasing a pair or more of the more common finches, like zebras, society finches, and gouldians. Other finches, like weavers or canaries, tend to be territorial and won't appreciate other birds in the cage with them when it's not breeding season.

If you put a male and a female together, and if they're society or zebra finches or another easily bred species (see Chapter 3 for more on the various finch species), you're fairly certain to have more finches in short order. You can refrain from providing a nest, but they'll try to breed in the food dish if it suits them.

If you don't want more finches, you do have a couple of options, however. In the absence of a member of the opposite sex, most zebra or society finches bond reasonably quickly with a member of the same sex. All birds or all bees — and no babies! Problem solved.

Most people keep two birds, let them breed once or twice a year, and find homes for the babies when the time comes. That seems to be the easiest way to go if you're certain you're ready for the responsibility of breeding the birds and finding suitable homes for their offspring.

If you choose to have an aviary with a number of pairs, perhaps including some of the babies you've raised yourself, be sure that they're pairing up such that they're not inbreeding. *Inbreeding* is when finches of the same family line breed together — siblings with siblings or parents with offspring. Sometimes, a hobby breeder will *line-breed,* using parent/offspring combinations to get a certain color or pattern in the babies, but they won't continue breeding this pair once the desired results have been achieved. Inbreeding isn't a good idea, because the babies may have health problems and may be weaker than birds that weren't inbred.

To prevent inbreeding, you have to separate the babies from the parents and from each other when they become mature. Or you can choose not to provide nests and hope that the birds don't decide to breed in the food dishes or on the bottom of the cage. If they breed once accidentally, don't fret — just don't let it happen again.

If you place different species in the same aviary, you'll want to be certain that they're compatible. You don't want to mix an aggressive species with a passive one. (See Chapter 3 for some information on which species tend to be more aggressive; when in doubt, talk with your avian veterinarian or other finch hobbyists.)

Chapter 3

Finding and Selecting a Finch

. . . .

. . . .

*F*inding your perfect pair of finches may seem easy at first glance. Just go to a pet store, right? Well, there's nothing wrong with doing just that. Nevertheless, knowing your choices *before* you see those particular birds you just can't live without is always a good idea. Almost any pet store that carries birds will have finches, but they may carry only the most common species, and perhaps you're looking for something a little more exotic.

Then again, you may have fallen in love with the first two finches you saw and brought them home on the spot. It happens to the best of us. A sweet little face and a soft song will steal your heart. Whatever the case, this chapter helps you choose your first finch — or your 50th.

Choosing Finches: Exploring Your Options

More than a thousand species of finches exist, though most of them are not available in the pet trade. Among these many different species are an absolutely marvelous number of *mutations* (including different color variations) to choose from. Different species have different personalities, too.

The common species of finches

At most pet shops, you'll be able to find some very commonly kept species of finches, including the ones in the following sections.

This is only a very small sampling of the available species. Dozens more are easily available as pets — and you can find even more with a little effort.

Zebra finches

Zebra finches are the most popular variety of companion finch today. In fact, they may very well be the most popular pet bird after the budgie and canary.

Native to the Australian grasslands, zebra finches are very hardy little birds and easy for a novice to handle. They're also easy for the novice to breed, and they rarely require any human intervention in the breeding process beyond providing a nest.

Dozens of color variations exist among zebra finches, but the "classic" zebra finch has black stripes on the chest and a red beak. The male has contrasting cheek patches, usually orange.

Zebras can be slightly aggressive at breeding time and occasionally have dominance issues in a larger group, especially if they're crowded.

Society finches

Society finches were actually created in captivity, first bred in China. Society finches never existed in the wild anywhere in the world. They're domesticated — entirely "made" by humans, the way dog breeds are — and descended from a few species of finches, though no one knows for sure which ones. As a result, they're the calmest finches around humans.

A society finch could be your best bet if you're determined to tackle the difficult task of finger-taming your finches (though this isn't recommended). Of all the varieties of finch, the society finch is the gentlest. They're pacifists by nature. If bullied by other birds, they'll generally back down. In addition, they often adopt the eggs or babies of another breeding pair and care for them as they would their own.

Needless to say, mixing society finches with other, more aggressive species is not a good idea, though they do well housed with zebra finches and Gouldian finches if given enough space.

Society finches were once known as the "little brown birds," but quite a variety of mutations exist today — though colors range only from white to dark brown or cinnamon. See Figure 3-1 for an example of a society finch.

© Isabelle Francais

Figure 3-1: Society finches are more colorful than "little brown birds."

Gouldian finches

The Lady Gouldian finch (or just *Gouldian finch,* for short) is prized mainly for its gorgeous plumage. Originating in Australia, this bird's stunning appearance is why people fancy these tiny creatures. This finch appears as if an artist got very creative with a palate full of colors — the best specimens of these birds don't even look real until you see them hopping from perch to perch. Gouldian finches are prime examples of the miracle and beauty of nature. They're found in a variety of dramatic colors. The males of this species are brighter than the female, making them easy to tell apart at maturity.

You'll probably find Gouldian finches with a bright red or a carrot-orange face, a green body, a blue head, a violet chest, a yellow belly, and a cobalt rump, though mutations do exist. For example, the blue Gouldian, which is primarily made up of shades of violet, blue, and white; still other mutations include shades of creams and browns.

Gouldian finches are tiny, but they make great aviary birds — they appreciate a large garden setting and add wonderful flashes of color to the foliage. As with most finches, the Gouldian is a quiet bird, hopping around and peeping. You may hear the male sing, but it is nothing like the song of a canary.

Gouldians are among the most difficult finch to breed. People who raise Gouldians usually also have society finches in a separate cage, and place the Gouldian's eggs in the society finch's nest. This ensures that the eggs and babies will get the proper care. When the babies arrive, you may be in for a shock — they're a dull grey-green and need a few months to mature to their full coloration.

Owl finches

The owl finch is a grass finch, also known as the Bicheno finch or the double-barred finch. Owl finches are a lively addition to a community aviary and a good choice if you don't have a lot of experience with birds.

This bird's native habitat is Australia, particularly the woodlands, grasslands, and scrublands, though they can also be found in city parks. They travel in groups numbering 4 to 40 and are active flyers.

In terms of coloration, the owl finch can't compete with the Gouldian or even the common zebra finch, but its distinctive markings and social disposition give it a character all its own. It stands between 3 and 4 inches in length and has two distinct black bars above and below a whitish-beige chest, one bar circling the underpart of the "chin" and the other rounding the bird's underside. The wings are brown with white speckles, and the face mask is white. The beak is gray and the eye is black.

The visual difference between the sexes is so slight that even owl-finch experts have a difficult time telling the males from the females. The males are said to have thicker bands and a whiter chest, though this is not always consistent. Males do have a soft, sweet song and females do not, so separating birds and listening for the song is one way of determining sex.

Owl finches are generally good parents, but some can be a little too carefree with their sitting habits or can toss the occasional baby out of the nest. Having other similarly sized finches — such as zebra finches and society finches — nesting at the same time is convenient, because they'll generally foster the eggs or babies willingly. Owl finches who are good parents will also foster other species as well. These birds absolutely need some direct natural light or artificial bird lighting to remain healthy. They often become darker or discolored if they aren't getting enough light.

European goldfinches

These birds have been kept as pets in Europe for many hundreds of years. They are very pretty — yellow, white, and gold, with a red face patch that is larger in the male than in the female. European goldfinches aren't as popular as canaries in the United States — probably because they're harder to breed — but they have a prettier and less repetitive song. Both male and female European goldfinches sing, but the females are not as intense as the males.

These birds are not recommended for novice keepers — but after you have some experience, they can be incredibly rewarding.

Whydah finches

Whydah finches, native to the tropics, are glossy black and pure white, which doesn't sound very spectacular, but they're truly striking in their appearance. During the breeding season, the male grows a spectacular tail that is often twice his own body length. When the breeding season is over, the male goes out of color and looks like an adult hen or a juvenile male.

The Whydah finch does not raise its own young, strangely enough. The female lays her eggs in another bird nest, each Whydah having a different "host" bird to call upon. The adoptive parents do the work for them, incubating the eggs and raising the Whydah chicks, often at the expense of their own babies.

These birds are not recommended for beginners, because they're hard to raise and can be aggressive to other birds their size.

The age of your new finches

You should probably look for young adult or newly weaned finches, especially if you're buying zebra or society finches (species that have been kept in captivity for a long time).

How can you tell how old a finch is? Generally speaking, baby finches wear a different color plumage than the adults, sometimes drastically different. Gouldian babies are a drab olive-green color, a far cry from their colorful parents. Baby java finches are dark gray with a charcoal-colored beak, not the stunning gray with white cheeks and pink beak of their parents. Baby zebra finches look like little gray sparrows — the bird is a drab brown and the beak is dark (you would never imagine that these birds turn into beautiful zebra finches).

Because finches mature so quickly, they're in adult feather by 3 to 6 months of age. At this point, knowing how old they are is difficult. Some breeders put a leg band on their babies when they're about 10 days old, and this band should have the year printed on it.

Finding a Finch

After you've made your checklist for your perfect pair of finches, you have to go out and find them. Fortunately, you can look in a variety of places, and if one place doesn't have what you're looking for, you can try another.

Pet shops

Most pet shops carry only the most popular varieties of finches, but as a first-time finch parent, you'll probably want to choose one of the popular species, anyway.

Here are some things to pay attention to when you walk into a pet shop for the first time:

- **When you walk in the door, pay attention to what your nose tells you.** If the store is dirty or smells funky, leave right away.

- **Look at the water in the birds' cage(s).** If the water is clean, that's a good sign — but if it looks like it came out of a muddy stock pond after a stampede, that's a major problem. Leave a store where the water isn't clean — but do the birds a favor and tell the manager on the way out.

- **Check for food in the birds' cage(s).** If the birds are out of food or if something is wrong with the food, leave. See the manager on your way out and alert him to the situation.

- **Look for too many birds in a cage.** Birds need room to move, and having too many birds in one cage is stressful for all the birds. Look for a pet store that doesn't pack its birds into cages like sardines in a can.

- **Look for birds that are inactive, that may look kind of puffy and/or be sleeping or standing on the floor of the cage, have puffy or swollen eyes or any dried or wet matter stuck to the feathers surrounding the vent.** These symptoms are indications of illness. Leave those birds alone.

- **Look for generally crowded conditions.** If all the bird cages are tightly stacked and crammed together, you can bet that, if one bird has an illness, the others are likely to get it, too.

- **Talk to the staff and see how helpful and knowledgeable they are.** If you ask for a zebra finch and the staff starts to put a Gouldian in a box for you, that isn't a good sign. Also, if the salespeople at your pet shop aren't friendly and helpful, they won't be friendly and helpful when you get home and have a problem, either.

Whether you buy from a general pet shop or a birds-only pet shop, be sure to ask some questions about your potential finches before you consider taking them home. Here's a good place to start:

- ✔ **Where do you get your finches?** If the answer is, "Some guy drops them off," reconsider buying from that store. If the answer is, "We get them from Breeder X who takes great care of his birds," that's a better answer — you can't be sure that it's the truth, but at least the store employee is trying. If the salesperson is very nice and says, "The owner breeds and hand-raises them herself — she's been a finch fancier for years," that's the best answer you can get.

- ✔ **Do these finches come with a health guarantee?** If the salesperson says, "What's that?" run fast and far away from the place. The store should be willing to take back the bird within a certain number of days if it doesn't get a clean bill of health from your avian veterinarian.

- ✔ **What are these finches eating?** "I dunno," is a terrible answer. "Seeds — what else would they eat?" is equally poor. If the answer is that all the birds are fed seeds or pellets plus fruits and vegetables and other fresh foods, you're likely to be happier with a bird from that store.

- ✔ **How old are these finches?** The store employees should be certain of the birds' ages.

Swap meets

You can often find finches sold at your local swap meet or flea market, but be aware that if you buy a pair of finches from a swap meet, you may not be able to find the person who sold them to you the very next week. Try to get a business card or a phone number when you purchase your bird.

The newspaper

Sometimes breeders advertise in the newspaper. The breeder may be a small-time home breeder with a few pairs and some babies to sell. This breeder may be a good choice because you may get to see where your bird came from and may even make a friend in the seller — a person who can help you if you have trouble with your finches.

Be careful about going to people's houses when you pick up your bird. Talk to the person on the phone a few times and take someone with you. Never go alone. Listen for birds in the background. If you don't hear any, be careful. Don't let the person come to your home either. Meeting in a safe, neutral place for the exchange is always a good idea. Odds are you won't have a problem, but remember that this is a stranger you've met from an ad in the newspaper.

Breeders and experts

If you're very lucky, you'll find an actual finch breeder — someone who breeds for color mutations and for showing. This person can even become a mentor to you, helping you become more knowledgeable in the hobby if you choose to breed your birds.

 When you arrive at the breeder's home, look for cleanliness and check to see if the birds are being treated humanely. Do they have enough space? Do they have fresh, clean water? Is the temperature too warm or too cold? If you feel comfortable with the conditions of the birds, then you should be comfortable buying one from this person.

 Again, ask for a health guarantee and the right to return your finches if they don't get a clean bill of health from your avian veterinarian.

Bird shows

If you're extremely lucky, you may find a bird show in your area. Very often avian breeders from around the country bring their birds to show and sell. A bird show is a great place to meet people and to see all kinds of different species and colors of finches.

 Walk around the show and talk to everyone. Take some numbers and make some friends. These people are the ones who know the most about your finches. They can help and advise you with any situation you may encounter.

Searching for a Healthy Finch

When you've decided on the color, age, gender, and type of finches you want, you now have to go about choosing a healthy pair — which is actually easier than you think. Check out the following sections for tips on what to look for in a healthy finch.

Eyes

A finch's eyes should be bright and shiny. No crust or discharge should be coming from the eyes. The eyes should not be puffy or swollen. A finch's eyes should show an attitude of alertness.

Nose and nares

A finch's nostrils are called *nares,* and they're located at the top of the beak where it meets the bird's face. The nares should be clean and without discharge.

Listen to the finch's breathing. If you hear a clicking noise, this could be indicative of air-sac mites — something you definitely want to avoid.

While you're looking, check for an overgrown beak, which is an indication of a problem.

Feathers

The feathers of a healthy finch are bright and shiny, lying flat against the body. A finch with excessively ruffled feathers may be ill, but this isn't always the case. Feathers can get ruffled if the bird is being picked on or if he has recently traveled in a small space with other finches.

Feathers should cover the whole body. If you notice bald patches, the finch has a problem — he may just have a feisty cage mate plucking a few of his feathers, but you can't be sure. Avoid finches with any bald patches.

Feet

A finch should have two feet (preferably), with four toes each (three forward and one back). The feet should be free of debris and any scaly patches, which may be a sign of mites. The finch should be able to perch easily on both feet.

Health guarantees

As with anything else, *buyer beware.* If you buy a bird without a health guarantee and your finch keels over, you're stuck with a dead finch and no recourse. Most good stores allow you a certain amount of time to take your bird for a checkup and will take the bird back if your avian vet finds a problem. If you buy a bird without a health guarantee, you're buying the bird at your own risk.

Vent

The *vent* is at the bottom of the bird and is the place where waste is eliminated and where eggs are laid. The vent should be clean and dry, not wet or crusted with feces or other material. You should also check for prolapse, which could be an indication that the bird has produced many eggs and is undoubtedly older than advertised.

A *prolapse* is when part of a bird's intestines or reproductive organs fall out of the *cloaca* (where eggs and feces come out). You'll easily be able to spot this if the finch you're looking at has it.

Attitude

Healthy finches are cheerful, alert, and busy, busy, busy — always on the move, interacting with cage mates, eating, flying, grooming one another, cuddling, quarreling, and mating. Their energy is incredible. If the bird you're looking at seems lethargic or tired, this could be an indication of trouble — or it could just be siesta time. Either way, before you commit to buying that particular bird, check back later to see if his energy level has increased.

You may well be tempted to buy the sleepy, sick looking bird. Of course, if you're a bird lover, how can you turn away from him? Do what feels right to you, but buying a sick bird is often a mistake. You risk infecting your other birds, you'll incur a huge veterinary bill, and the bird may not survive anyway. You're better off starting out with a healthy bird that will cause you the least worries.

Chapter 4

Home Tweet Home: Preparing for Your Finch and Bringing It Home

*W*hen you've found your perfect pair of finches, you're going to need to get ready to bring them to their new home, and that involves a lot more than just putting them in a cage and leaving them some food and water. This chapter shows you some of the ways to house your finches and how to accessorize your finches' home so that they stay happy and healthy.

Housing Finches Together

Try not to house a finch alone for long. Most finches definitely like to be in pairs, though some are territorial and won't want to be housed with other finches when it's not breeding season.

That said, don't crowd them. If you want to house more than one pair, increase your cage size accordingly. Also, if you're planning to mix species of finches, talk with an experienced breeder to determine which species can live together and which species interfere with each other when breeding. Each pair of finches should have at least 2 square feet of space to themselves.

Some pairings known to work — and not work — include the following:

- Society finches do very well with zebra finches, parrot finches, cordon bleus, cherry finches, Whydah finches, strawberry finches, and Gouldian finches.

- Gouldian finches can be housed with zebra finches if your aviary is large enough, though zebras may interfere with the Gouldian finches' breeding.

- Zebra and society finches can be housed with non-aggressive parrot species such as budgies, Bourke's parakeets, and cockatiels, but there must be enough room in the aviary for all of them to get out of the way of each other and to nest when they choose.

- Weaver finches should not be housed with any other type of finches.

- Canaries can only be housed together when they're breeding. Otherwise, they should be kept in separate cages.

Your Finches' New Home

Very few finches are *finger tame,* which means that giving them opportunities to fly free in your home requires effort, preparation, and time — and those opportunities may not come all that often. You don't always have an afternoon to spend catching your wandering finches, after all. Chances are that your finches will spend the majority of their time in their cage or aviary. No cage can ever replace flying free, but the more spacious you can make it for them, the better.

Finches need to fly for exercise, and if their cage is too small for them to fly from perch to perch, their health will eventually suffer.

Size is everything

At an absolute minimum, a cage for a single pair of finches should measure 36 inches in length, by 24 inches in width, by 18 inches in height — but that is strictly a minimum. Instead, look for the absolute largest cage that the space in your home and your budget will allow. The horizontal dimensions (the dimensions across) are more important than the height. ***Remember:*** Your birds *must* fly to stay healthy.

Long, rectangular cages are better than round cages for finches. Finches won't take advantage of the height of the cage as much as they will the back-and-forth flying space.

Regardless of the size of the cage, the spacing of the bars or mesh still matters. Most popular finches are tiny creatures, and they can be seriously hurt or killed by getting stuck or hung between the bars of a cage. The spacing should never be greater than ¼ inch between the bars.

When you're ready for your feathered family to grow, you may want to consider an aviary. An *aviary* is a huge cage designed to hold several pairs of finches. An aviary can be situated inside your home or outside, and it should be large enough for a human being to enter. An aviary affords your birds a far greater opportunity to fly than a standard cage does, and it allows your finches to follow their natural group-living instinct. An aviary also lets you make your finches' home a lot more interesting. You can add more types of perches and some nontoxic natural tree branches. If you're planning to do any serious breeding and raise a lot of birds, you'll certainly need an aviary, but considering one even if you're not breeding them is a good idea.

Habitats are generally much larger than aviaries, and they mimic the species' natural environment as much as possible. In addition to plants, habitats usually include running water. Habitats are nearly always located outside, giving your finches an opportunity to enjoy some fresh air and sunshine.

Take care when you house your birds outdoors to protect them from predators and weather. Non-tropical finches can live outdoors year-round, but they must be acclimated to the weather by being outside when the seasons change. If you keep them inside where it's warm and then put them outside in the extreme cold, the temperature change can be shocking for them and they may die. Finches can even handle snow and ice, but they have to be the species of finches that come from climates where winters are similar to yours.

A good rule is that your finches should be housed in the same basic temperature as they would in their native wild habitat.

Considering cage materials

Metal and plastic cages are suitable for finches, as long as they're constructed with nontoxic materials and contain no zinc (no "galvanized" metal). Be wary of the coatings used to cover metal cages. If it starts to flake and your birds ingest it, they can become extremely ill and even die.

Quarantine: When, where, why, and how

When one of your birds is ill or when you introduce a new bird to your home or aviary, you should establish a quarantine procedure. In the case of new birds, this is a matter of putting them into a different room, far from your other birds for a period of 40 days — you don't want to risk exposing your other birds to a potentially fatal illness. Some people quarantine for 30 days with good results. If you do notice something wrong with your finches, seek veterinary care for them immediately.

Separate a sick bird from your other birds as well. Place it in a hospital cage by itself, in a location where it won't be disturbed. To create a hospital cage, use a 10-gallon aquarium. Provide a mild heat source — a heating pad or lamp placed under or on one-half of the cage that brings the temperature inside the cage to about 90° F (32° C). Make sure that the bird is able to move away from the heat source if it becomes too warm. Check the cage several times to be sure that your bird isn't too warm. If the bird is too sick to get around the cage well, place food and water on the floor of the cage, where the bird can get to it easily, and make sure the water dish is very shallow — if the water dish isn't shallow, you risk the bird drowning. A quarter inch of water should be fine.

Maintain the finch's normal daylight/nighttime schedule if possible. If you normally cover your birds at night, you should cover the ill one, too, but make sure that your heating source will not make it too warm with the cage covered.

If price is no object, you may want to look into some of the wood and acrylic cages available these days. Some of them are exquisite furniture and help to eliminate a lot of mess. Of course, their prices reflect that.

Wooden pagoda-type cages are unacceptable for finches. Although they're very popular, they tend to harbor moisture, bacteria, and fungus, and they can even be home to parasites that may affect your birds. Stick with materials that are easier to clean.

Keeping safety in mind

Finches are surprisingly hardy, but they can be fragile, too. Fancy or elaborate metalwork on a cage can catch a tiny toe and break it or tear the nail. Scrollwork and round cages with bars that taper together as they reach the top (see Figure 4-1) pose a choking hazard if a bird gets her head caught.

Figure 4-1: Avoid cages that have bars that taper together.

The cage bottom should have some kind of mesh or grating about ½ inch or more above the liner. This is to keep the birds from walking around in their own mess. The best liner for the bottom of the cage is plain old newspaper. The ink has disinfectant properties, and you can easily see how much mess needs to be cleaned up.

You may be tempted to use bird litter, but I don't recommend it. When you use litter, seeing if one of your birds has a problem or if the cage needs cleaning is made more difficult, and the litter also holds moisture, which allows bacteria and fungus to grow.

Deciding where to put your bird's cage

Your finches will be happiest with their primary residence against a solid wall or in a corner. If you can't find a location like this, cover one side of the cage with something solid, like a very heavy dark cloth. Finches feel very insecure and frightened if they're out in the open and can't get away because they're trapped in a cage.

Finches are a prey bird, always on the lookout for the approach of a predator. With a solid surface or two to make them feel protected, they'll relax and settle in far more readily.

Place the cage in an area that will see a bit of activity — but not too much activity. Your finches are stimulated by watching things happen in the room, but they'll be uneasy if they're too much in the middle of it.

Small, tropical finches are susceptible to colds. Place the cage well away from any drafts. Ideally, the room where they live should remain at a constant temperature. Choose a spot that gets a lot of ambient light during the day, preferably natural light. The location should also be a quiet place during the night hours. A small amount of direct sunlight is very good for your birds' health, but they should be able to escape from it if they want — direct sunlight can get much too hot for them very quickly.

There are some places where you should *never* place your finches' cage. These include the following:

- ✔ **The floor:** A high spot will make your finches feel safe. A low spot will make them uneasy, especially if you have other pets.

- ✔ **The hallway:** Hallways have too much traffic.

- ✔ **A child's bedroom:** Small children should only interact with finches under close supervision. These tiny birds are too easily injured to survive being handled by a small child.

- ✔ **The bathroom:** The temperature and humidity fluctuate too much here.

- ✔ **The kitchen:** Kitchens have lots of temperature changes, and the fumes given off by nonstick cookware are deadly to birds. (Avoid nonstick cookware even if your birds are in another area of the house — fumes can easily travel through walls.)

- ✔ **Directly in front of a window:** Your birds will be frightened by neighborhood cats and anything else unfriendly that passes by. The headlights of cars may frighten them, as will the sun bouncing off cars' windshields. Even more important, too much direct sunlight can make the cage far too warm.

Accessorizing Your Finches' Abode

Finches need a few specific accessories to keep them happy and healthy. However, make sure not to clutter a cage so much that your birds cannot fly back and forth. With that in mind, here are some things that your finches need.

Something to stand on

Your cage probably came with a couple of perches, and they're fine, but variety is important. Your birds spend a lot of time on their feet, so they need a variety of materials, widths, and textures to stand on to keep their feet healthy.

Be sure not to position perches above food and water dishes, and leave plenty of room in the cage for unobstructed flight. If you crowd the cage, your finches may injure themselves flying into the perches in a panic.

Wooden perches

Not all wooden perches are just plain pine dowels (see Figure 4-2). Manzanita perches come in some unusual shapes, and cholla wood is nicely textured. You may even want to use a branch cut from one of your own trees, with the bark still on it — as long as you're sure the wood is nontoxic and has never been sprayed with insecticide or fungicide. The rough coating of bark is good for your finches' feet, and it will also help to keep their claws worn down. Most hardwoods are safe, as are pine and fruit trees, such as citrus, plum, pear, and apple.

Figure 4-2: Your finches will enjoy natural wooden perches of varying sizes.

Mites and moths and birds, oh my!

A *mite protector* is a small can that hangs on your birds' cage and contains an insecticide. It isn't very healthy for your birds, and isn't necessary either. Though your birds can pick up mites, if you keep the cage clean, visit your veterinarian often, and observe a quarantine period for any new birds introduced into your household, they're unlikely to develop a serious problem.

The *seed moth* is a type of moth that sometimes arrives in bulk seed. It won't harm your birds, but if you find that you have a problem in a batch of bulk seed, put the seed in the freezer. Protect your other dry goods by putting them in plastic bags or containers, and then purchase a trap that attracts the moths using their own *pheromones,* which are kind of like hormones that the other insects can smell.

The drawback to wooden perches is that they require frequent cleaning. Wood absorbs biological materials that decompose and can grow colonies of bacteria. Wooden perches need to be scrubbed thoroughly at least once a week. About every ten days, soak them in a 10 percent solution of chlorine bleach and water (9 cups water to 1 cup bleach). Be sure the perches are thoroughly rinsed and completely dry before returning the perches to the cage.

Plastic perches

Plastic perches, like the ones that probably came with your cage, are very easy to clean and snap on and off at various places around your cage. However, they're probably not as comfortable for your finches as natural wood.

Rope perches

Rope perches have traditionally been used for parrots, but several brands of tightly twisted cotton rope perches are made especially for finches. You want tightly twisted rope perches so that they won't snag your finches' tiny claws.

Cups and bowls

Plastic is not a great choice for your food and water dishes. It scratches easily and retains bacteria in the crevasses. Instead, opt for ceramic or stainless steel. Stainless steel is outstanding because it's easy to clean, hygienic, and absolutely safe for your birds. Both ceramic and stainless steel dishes are available with the hardware to snap in and out of the cage.

If your finches throw enough seeds out of the cage to make it sound like Lawrence of Arabia is striding across the sand when you walk through your living room, you should consider a seed dish with a hood. Your finches can fling away, but without dumping the entire cup of seeds.

Buy two complete sets of dishes for your birds, and you'll have a much easier time keeping them clean. Soak one set in a 10 percent bleach solution while the other is in use and make sure to rinse thoroughly before using them again.

A special type of cup is made to hold one half of a boiled egg, an outstanding treat for your finches. Feeding finches quite a lot of egg when they're breeding is important, so this cup is especially useful at those times.

Some people really like tube-style waterers for finches because the water often stays cleaner longer in the tube and there is less area for the birds to toss food and droppings. However, just because the water lasts longer doesn't mean you don't have to change it every day.

Cage covers

Most birds feel more secure having their cage covered at night — and finches are no exception. A cover provides darkness and protects finches from nighttime movement in the house — perhaps a cat slinking about in the night, or mice scuttling around. The cover also protects finches from drafts, and the darkness inside the cage may allow you to sleep a little longer if your birds like rising with the sun.

Make sure that the cage doesn't become too warm with the cover in place. Also, be sure that your finches don't develop *night frights,* a kind of birdy panic attack that generally happens when they hear or see things at night that frighten them. If they do panic at night, and they thrash around the cage, cover only three of the four sides of the cage so that the birds have a bit of light. A nightlight is also a good idea.

Mineral blocks and cuttlebones

A cuttlebone is an absolutely necessity for your finches. It's the bone from a type of squid, and it provides a great source of calcium. A mineral block is also a good source of calcium and helps your finches keep their beaks trimmed.

Toys

Typical finches are not as interested in toys as parrots are, but because they spend most of their lives in a cage, giving them some interesting things to do is a good idea.

With finches, the key is to keep it simple. Small ladders and swings, a small bell, and a mirror should do the trick.

Be careful with mirrors. You'll enjoy watching your finches interact with that "other" bird, but if your birds start to feel that their territory is being violated, they can become stressed. If your finches attack the mirror, remove it from the cage.

Baths

Your finches need to bathe. Bathing keeps their feathers and skin in good condition, and it improves their sense of well-being. Most finches bathe several times a week, sometimes every day, even when breeding. The eggs need moisture to remain healthy (yes, eggs need to be healthy!), so the female will bathe and bring moisture back to the nest on her feathers.

Before deciding on a bathing setup, remember that birds drown very easily. They don't need to immerse themselves to get a bath — in fact, giving them a bathing arrangement that's too deep is dangerous. A flat, shallow dish with about ½ inch of water in it is perfect for finches. Your finches will wade in it, splash in it, flutter their wings, and scatter droplets in it. Your finches will also cheerfully drink their bathwater despite having a separate water dish, so change their bathwater daily.

Once in a while, and only if they seem to enjoy it, you can spray your finches gently with a fine mist from a spray bottle. If they like this gentle misting, they'll let you know by lifting a wing and turning this way and that to get the spray right where they want it.

Lighting

If you live in a cold part of the country, or if you aren't able to provide your finches with direct sunlight, you can purchase a bird lamp with a broad-spectrum light bulb, one that's made specially for birds or reptiles. Or you can put the bulb in an ordinary cheap spotlight that you purchase at any hardware store. These lights do a pretty good job of imitating sunlight — they aren't perfect, but they're better than nothing.

Your birds need this broad-spectrum light to synthesize vitamins and remain healthy. If your pet store doesn't carry bulbs made especially for birds, a bulb made for reptiles will work just fine. If your birds are breeding, they'll need either sunlight or full-spectrum light about 14 hours per day.

Keeping Mess Away

Even if you have only one pair of finches, the mess in your home may multiply. These busy little darlings find some truly inventive ways to scatter mess. Take heart. You can get the situation under control without resorting to demolition or a servant staff.

Cage bloomers and seed guards

Cage bloomers and seed guards both fit around the bottom of the cage and help to keep the scattered seeds and vegetables where they belong — in the cage tray.

If your birds are truly talented at seed flinging, bloomers and guards may not be enough. One method that seems to work is to purchase some clear plastic from a fabric shop and cover the back and sides of the cage with it, leaving the top and front open to the air. You may even need to put a small flap of plastic in front where the food and water dishes sit.

Cleaning supplies

One of the most important investments you can make is a small hand vacuum. If you leave one of these little hand vacuums a few feet from your finches' cage, contending with mess is a lot easier.

Most things you're accustomed to using to clean up stubborn messes are toxic to your feathered friends. Instead, try the all-natural route: Baking soda makes an excellent scrubber, and vinegar is an outstanding disinfectant. But don't use them together — the chemical reaction is quite startling.

If you're lacking in the spirit of cleaning adventure, your pet shop sells several safe-for-birds cleansers that do a fair job and smell pretty good. But you'll still need to do some scrubbing.

Change the paper in the bottom of the cage daily or at least every other day. Scrape off dried droppings once a week. About every ten days, soak the entire cage in soapy water and disinfect in a 10-percent chlorine bleach solution. Rinse and dry thoroughly before returning your feathered friends to their home. You can certainly clean more often than this, but this is a good place to start.

Finch-Proofing Your Home

If you plan to allow your finches free-flight time, even if you think that you're going to supervise them all the time, you have to finch-proof your home. Even if you have a pair that's *never* going to leave the cage, the average home has things that can be harmful, even deadly, to little finches.

Here are a few tips to keep your birds safe:

- ✔ **Make sure all windows are screened.** Finches are excellent fliers.

- ✔ **Remove frilly, lacy curtains.** A finch can hang a tiny claw in them and become trapped and injured. If you don't see it happen, the bird could go into a full-blown panic attack and die.

- ✔ **Keep your windows and mirrors a little dirty.** Yep, you heard me right. Windows and mirrors should be covered, be a little dirty, or have stickers on them, because your finches may mistake the glass for open space and fly into it.

- ✔ **Get rid of the ceiling fan.** Your finches may fly up there while it's on. Enough said.

- ✔ **Eliminate from your house all substances that produce fumes or scents.** Finches have an extremely delicate respiratory system. Fumes that may not bother you — like those from a scented candle or an air freshener — can kill a finch. When it's heated, nonstick cookware also emits fumes that are proven to kill birds. (See the list later in this section for information on which common household products include this coating and should be avoided at all costs.)

- ✔ **Put all medications out of reach of your finches.** Those pills may look like tempting treats for your finch — and the result could be deadly.

- ✔ **Make sure your finch can't access standing water.** Water such as that of a fish tank poses a drowning threat to a finch. A finch can even drown in a glass of water while trying to take a drink.

- ✔ **Remove all toxic houseplants from your finches' reach.** Quite a large number of common houseplants are dangerous for your finches. These include — but are definitely not limited to — bird of paradise, daffodil, hyacinth, mistletoe, and all types of ivy. A complete list of toxic plants would need a volume of its own, so if you have questions about any plants, ask your veterinarian.

✔ **Keep predators away.** Although you may not think of them as predators, your companion cat or dog or ferret can be very dangerous for your finches. Your hungry cat is always thinking of ways to get close to your finch, and dogs have a strong prey drive as well. If you keep your finches outside, they can become prey to raccoons, opossums, hawks, and other predators. Make sure that all outdoor cages are double-wired to prevent other animals from getting in.

✔ **Keep temperature changes to a minimum.** Your finches come from a wide variety of climates and can adapt to a reasonably wide range of temperatures if they're in good health. In any case, avoid rapid changes in temperature and drafts. If your finches are overheated, mist them with cool water and position a fan so it's blowing near them, but not on them. If they're too chilled, immediately warm them up in a hospital cage (see the sidebar "Quarantine: When, where, why, and how," earlier in this chapter, for tips on creating a hospital cage using an aquarium).

✔ **Use a bedspread with a very tight weave.** Bedclothes are a good place for your finches to get tangled up and hurt.

✔ **If your furniture has any loose-weave upholstery, cover it.** Your finches may get hung in the weave and injured.

Products that use nonstick coating (and that should be avoided at all costs) include the following:

✔ Anything that says it is "nonstick"

✔ Bread machines

✔ Broiler pans

✔ Coffeemakers

✔ Nonstick cooking utensils

✔ Crock pots

✔ Curling irons

✔ Deep fryers

✔ Drip pans for burners

✔ Electric skillets

✔ Griddles

✔ Hair dryers (with nonstick coating inside)

✔ Heat lamps

✔ Ironing-board covers

✔ Irons

✔ Lollipop molds

✔ Pizza pans

✔ Popcorn poppers

✔ Portable heaters

✔ Roasters

✔ Rolling pins (the nonstick variety)

✔ Stockpots

✔ Stovetop burners

✔ Waffle makers

✔ Woks

Going Safely from Store to Home

If you buy your finches at a pet store, they'll send you home with your finches in a temporary carrier that resembles a cardboard box. You're going to need to purchase a travel cage anyway — you'll need to transport your birds to and from the veterinarian, and you may need a safe place for them while you're doing a thorough cleaning on their cage — so you may as well buy a travel cage when you buy your finches. Temporary quarters for your little ones do not have to be as large as their permanent home, but you don't want to have to stuff them into it with a shoehorn either.

If your birds will be in the travel carrier for a long time, you may want to supply a dish of seed and some oranges cut in half. You can offer them water for a few minutes every couple of hours, but don't leave water in the travel cage while you're driving. It could spill and make your birds miserable until they dry off again.

Don't use perches inside the travel cage. Finches can fly into the perches and get injured. Also, perches may injure finches if the birds are being jostled around in a moving car. Your finches will be fine on the bottom of the carrier.

When you're driving, make sure that the travel cage isn't sitting in direct sunlight — finches can be overcome by heat very quickly. If the weather is chilly, bring a towel and cover the carrier with it. Never leave the birds in the car in extreme temperatures, below 50° F (10° C) or above 90° F (32° C). If the temperature is warm, be sure the bird has water at all times.

Chapter 5

Caring for Your Finch

- -

In This Chapter

▶ Knowing what your finch needs and wants to eat

▶ One, two . . . one, two: Exercising your finch

▶ Putting your finch to sleep for the night

▶ Helping your finch get along with other pets

- -

*Y*ou've brought your finches home, and you've prepared a nice home for them. Now what? In addition to the many hours of pleasure you can expect in watching your feathered companions, you're also going to have some responsibilities. Finches are very complex and active creatures, and they have some definite needs. No, you won't have to spend 24 hours a day caring for them, but you will need to do some things correctly if you want your companions to be happy and healthy.

Water: Extremely Essential

Like all living creatures, finches need an ample supply of clean drinking water. In the wild, the search for water takes up a great deal of a finch's time and energy.

Besides providing plenty of water, in the case of caged or aviary finches, keep in mind the following suggestions:

✔ **Place a variety of water dishes in different locations in the cage at all times to minimize competition and quibbling among birds.** A bully finch may not let another, meeker finch drink, and this can be deadly.

✔ **Place at least one water dish in the lower part of the cage so that a bird who may be feeling a little under the weather**

doesn't have to fly to a perch to drink. Finches can become dehydrated to a life-threatening degree in a matter of just a few hours, so if you're busy or preoccupied for a relatively short period and fail to notice that one of your birds isn't getting to the water dish, this can be fatal.

✔ **Use either bottled drinking water or filtered tap water — but never water straight from the tap.** The additives in tap water are not good for your finches (or for you, for that matter). Filtered tap water is the cheapest solution over time, but make sure that the filter is a good one. The best, but most expensive option, is bottled drinking water. *Remember:* Your finches won't make a distinction between their bathing and drinking water, so their bathing water should come from a filtered source also, and it should be as clean as their drinking water (see Figure 5-1).

✔ **Change all water in your finches' cage or aviary at least once daily.** Two or three times per day is even better, especially if you pass the cage and it looks like your birds have had a mud fight in their water dishes.

Making water changes is easiest if you have multiple sets of water dishes and rotate them morning and evening or more often, if necessary. Soak the dishes in a 10-percent bleach solution once a week and rinse thoroughly before replacing them in your finches' cage.

Even if you use a tube waterer, change water daily to keep your companions' water clean and free of bacteria and filth. It doesn't matter what the package says — a two-week waterer still has to be changed daily!

Figure 5-1: Change bathing and drinking water daily.

Knowing What Your Finch Should (and Shouldn't) Eat

The most important thing to understand when it comes to feeding your finches is that finches actually have two diets — one for the breeding season and one for the non-breeding season. The differences are minor but extremely important.

Ideally, you want your finches to have a diet as close to their natural diet in the wild as possible. This means offering a wide variety of carbohydrate and protein sources. In the following sections, I fill you in on which foods and supplements are good to add during breeding.

What to feed your finch

Seed and pellets are only the beginning. In the wild, your birds would also have access to a variety of vegetation and live insects. Though most finches can survive for a while on seed alone, they are unlikely to thrive or breed on such a diet.

In the following sections, I tell you which foods your finch will favor.

Seeds and pellets

Finches come from all over the world, so obviously, what they eat in different locations is different. Each species likes a slightly different seed mix for this reason. Goldfinches, for example, like a mixture of canary seed, niger, rape, and hemp; zebras and society finches prefer a mix of yellow, white, and panicum millets, Japanese millet, spray millet, and small canary seed. Many commercial mixes of finch seed are available.

All labels show ingredients, and some labels indicate the species the seed is best for. A little checking of labels will show you the mix ideal for your finches.

If you notice that your finches regularly leave a certain type of seed in their dish and voraciously eat other types, you'll begin to get an idea of what your finches like. Buying seeds that your birds don't eat is a waste of money. Instead, you can make your own mix by buying in bulk the seeds they like.

Don't be taken in by highly priced, specially fortified seeds with vitamins and pretty colors. These mixtures have extra vitamins in the coating on the shell or husk of the seed. Because finches don't eat the husk, the vitamins don't do them any good.

Some people recommend substituting specially formulated pellets for seeds, but pellets are different enough from your finches' natural diet that you may have considerable difficulty convincing your finches that the pellets are for eating. Finches nearly always prefer real seeds, but there is certainly no harm in offering pellets.

Be certain that whatever pellets are offered are formulated for finches, and never, ever make the birds go cold turkey when changing them from seeds to pellets. Instead, mix the seeds and pellets and change the ratio of seeds to pellets gradually so that, eventually, all you're serving is pellets. *Remember:* Finches can die if they don't have food for several hours, so don't starve them.

Because your finches hull their seeds, it will often look like a whole bowl of seeds is waiting to be eaten, when in reality what you're seeing is just hulls – the part of the seed that the bird leaves behind after it eats the inside. Even if you see a "full bowl" of seeds, adding new seeds every day is important.

Veggies and fruit

Veggies, especially dark green and orange ones, are wonderful for your finches. These contain vitamin A, an essential nutrient. Fruits in these colors are wonderful as well. The more variety, the better. Try offering fruits and veggies chopped, shredded, cooked, and mashed — you can even clip washed greens to the side of the cage or weave them in between the bars. Make sure to wash everything very well before you feed it.

Birds are individuals, just like people, and their likes and dislikes vary widely. Some things your birds may love include grated Brussels sprouts, grated carrots, shredded romaine lettuce, kale, spinach, cucumber, melon, broccoli heads, alfalfa sprouts, wholewheat bread, and cornbread.

Here's a list of vegetables that are good for your finch:

- ✔ Beet tops
- ✔ Beets (raw or cooked)
- ✔ Bell pepper
- ✔ Broccoli
- ✔ Brussels sprouts

- ✔ Carrots (raw or cooked)
- ✔ Celery
- ✔ Chard
- ✔ Collard greens
- ✔ Corn

- ✔ Dandelion asparagus
- ✔ Endive
- ✔ Green beans
- ✔ Green pepper
- ✔ Jalapenos
- ✔ Kale
- ✔ Mustard greens

- ✔ Pumpkin
- ✔ Spinach
- ✔ Watercress peas
- ✔ Yams (cooked)
- ✔ Yellow squash
- ✔ Zucchini

Never leave fresh foods in your birds' cage for very long. Two hours to about half a day should do, depending on the weather. If you live in a warm climate (or it's summertime), make sure that fresh foods don't spoil.

An extremely easy thing to do is to buy a bag of frozen mixed vegetables at the supermarket and thaw small amounts daily for your birds. Frozen veggies aren't as good as fresh ones, but they're great when you're busy. Chop them into fine pieces so that they're easier for your finches to eat.

Most finches love fruits. Fruits are excellent sources for some of the vitamins your little companions need. Some things to try include bits of apple, banana, pear, honeydew, cantaloupe, grapes (with skin), peaches, plums, and figs. If you like it, your birds probably will, too.

Make sure that fruit is always fresh. Don't leave fruit in your birds' cage overnight.

Here's a list of fruits that are good for your finch:

- ✔ Apples
- ✔ Apricots
- ✔ Bananas
- ✔ Berries (any variety)
- ✔ Cantaloupe
- ✔ Cherries
- ✔ Figs
- ✔ Grapefruit
- ✔ Grapes
- ✔ Honeydew melon

- ✔ Kiwi
- ✔ Mango
- ✔ Oranges
- ✔ Papaya
- ✔ Peaches
- ✔ Pears
- ✔ Pineapple
- ✔ Plums
- ✔ Watermelon

Snacks

You can have a good deal of fun with your birds when it comes to snacks. Preparing healthful treats for your finches is fun. When those treats are good for them, watching them go wild over some-thing new and particularly tasty is even *more* fun.

Finches dearly love hard-boiled egg. Egg is an important source of protein and vitamins for them, especially when they're breeding. Mash up a bit of very-well-cooked hard-boiled egg and put it in one of their dishes. I guarantee a show! Include the shells — they're a great source of calcium. When you make eggs, rinse the eggshells thoroughly, microwave them for 4 minutes or bake them at 350° F (175° C) for 45 minutes (to kill salmonella, which is as deadly for your birds as it is for you), dry them, crush them, and offer them in a separate dish. Eggs provide an important source of calcium, and your birds will go wild for them.

A millet spray is another fun treat. Though seeds are part of your finches' staple diet, the process of figuring out how to get them out of a millet spray tied to the side of the cage affords lots of enjoyment for both you and your birds.

Live insects

Your finches need protein. In the wild, they obtain much of their protein from live insects, and they should ideally receive live insects from you, especially when they're breeding. The easiest way to pro-vide this is with commercially purchased insects. You can breed them yourself, but few people want to go through this trouble — though it's a fun project for school kids. Mealworms are very easy to raise, and you get the benefit of being able to feed them to your finches when they're very small and soft.

Your choices include mini-mealworms, waxworms, white worms, fruit flies, maggots, and fruit-fly larvae. When your finches are not breeding, offer them live insects two to three times per week if you can. During the breeding season, your finches will need some live insects daily.

Table foods

If you exercise a little common sense, your birds will enjoy and ben-efit from almost anything that you can eat. With the exception of a few things (which I outline later in this chapter), they can have some of just about everything on your plate.

Obviously, you should avoid feeding them some foods, but the ones you should avoid are not good for you either. Avoid excessive salt, foods that are very fatty or greasy — the sorts of things that your doctor tells you to avoid. Soft whole-wheat bread is great, as are crumbled wheat crackers, as long as they aren't salted.

Offer pound cake in tiny amounts to your finches on a semiregular basis (to get them used to eating it)! You should avoid sugars almost all the time, but pound cake is a superior way to get your finches to take medicines when they need them. You can soak the pound cake in the medication and then feed it to the birds.

Cooked foods

Several companies now offer cooked food for various species of birds, including finches. Generally, these are excellent diets for birds — easy and convenient.

Most cooked foods for birds expand when cooked, some as much as 100 percent. Check the labels carefully so you don't prepare too much. You can refrigerate cooked food for a few days, but it will go bad soon after that.

You can also make cornbread just for your finches, adding pellets, peas, and most anything else they like. You can make whole-wheat pasta and melt soy cheese over it if you want to get really inventive.

What not to feed your finch

Here is a list of the things you must keep your little hungry companions away from:

- ✔ **Chocolate:** Chocolate is toxic for birds.
- ✔ **Avocado:** This tasty plant harbors an ingredient near the skin of its pit that is toxic to birds.
- ✔ **Onions:** Onions aren't good for finches.
- ✔ **Alcohol:** Never allow your finch to sip an alcoholic beverage.
- ✔ **Pits and fruit seeds:** Some pits and fruit seeds are dangerous. Don't take the chance. Remove them from fruits before offering to your finches.
- ✔ **Mushrooms:** Not good for finches.
- ✔ **Spinach and chard:** These are fine foods for your finches when it's not breeding season. Though they have many nutritious vitamins in them, they also have an acid in them that binds calcium, making it unusable in the body — and when finches are in breeding season, they need calcium.

✔ **Salt:** Salt is toxic for finches — and it isn't very good for you, either.

✔ **Caffeine:** Caffeine is not good for birds and can be toxic.

The best general rule is to avoid junk foods. Keep your finch well away from the foods your doctor tells you to avoid yourself.

Nutritional supplements: When food is not enough

All finches should have a cuttlebone available, tied to the side of their cage, because it provides a constant and reliable source of calcium and keeps their beaks in good shape.

You may choose to provide your finches with additional vitamin supplements, although if your birds eat a sufficiently varied and nutritious diet, supplements shouldn't be necessary.

In some cases, too high a dosage of vitamins can be as bad for your bird as a deficiency. Always follow the instructions for dosage on any supplement you administer to your birds. When in doubt, ask your avian veterinarian.

The most common type of vitamin and mineral supplements for finches is a liquid supplement to add to their water. Liquid vitamin supplements can cause your finches' water dishes to become a breeding ground for some dangerous types of bacteria. Change water dosed with supplements more frequently. In addition, don't sprinkle liquid supplements over seeds, because this will cause the seeds to become rancid very quickly.

Some very good food supplements are on the market, and you can add these to your finches' daily diet. But you have to be sure to use them correctly to get the most benefit from them.

Don't put powdered supplements directly on seed. Your birds hull their seeds, and in the course of doing this, all the powder will probably end up in the bottom of the seed dish rather than inside your birds. Instead, sprinkle powdered supplements on mini-mealworms or veggies and fruits.

A heated controversy exists within the bird community on whether or not to offer your finches any type of grit. They probably won't need grit to digest their foods. On the other hand, ground oyster shell and crushed (and sterilized) eggshells are important sources of calcium for your finches. With other forms of grit, such as crushed charcoal or sand, the finch may overeat and the grit could become impacted inside your feathered friend's gut, which can be life threatening. If you talk to five different finch experts, you'll get five different opinions on whether you should offer grit to your finches and how much you should offer. The safest solution is to discuss this at length with your avian veterinarian or other finch hobbyists in your area.

Helping Your Finches Get the Exercise They Need

Finches fly all day long inside their cages, which is the reason that large cages are so essential for these birds. If the cage is large, particularly the horizontal dimension, and contains room for flight between perches without anything in the way, your birds don't ever need to leave their cage.

You may want to allow your finches to enjoy free flight from time to time as a treat. If you do this, be certain that the environment is safe for your finches. Watch for loose-weave upholstery items, frilly curtains, standing water, and other things that could harm your birds.

You'll also need to explore safe ways of catching your finches to return them to their cage or aviary. Many pet shops sell a variety of nets for this purpose. Another technique, usable at night, is to note the location of your finch or finches and simply turn off the light. You should be able to catch a finch quite easily and gently by hand in a darkened room.

The easiest way to get your finches in their cages when you let them fly free is to leave the cage door open and offer an especially enticing treat, like millet spray, for them at the end of their exercise period.

Getting a Good Night's Sleep: Putting Your Finch to Bed

The key to a good night's sleep is darkness and natural silence (in other words, the regular noises of night, not the television or ringing phone). Most people cover their finches' cage at night, which usually keeps them quiet and safe. It also protects them from drafts and helps to keep anything from disturbing your birds.

Some finches don't like being covered and may become frightened and agitated by unseen movement in the room. If that happens, cover only a portion of the cage, so that your finches still have a good view of the room, and use a dim nightlight near the cage.

One advantage with a good cage cover is that your finches' cage will remain dark for a longer period in the early morning and may prevent your finches from waking with the sun and tweeting you and your family right out of bed.

Grooming Your Finch

Grooming your finch isn't like grooming a dog or even a parrot. You don't have a lot to do with the grooming process — you can pretty much leave it to the finches.

Toenail clipping

Any bird's toenails can become unpleasantly sharp and overgrown and may require clipping. Sharp nails can get caught in rope or nesting material and can harm eggs in the nest. You can minimize overgrown nails by maintaining several perches in your finches' cage that are rough in surface texture, like concrete.

The first hurdle to clipping your finch's toenails is catching the bird. An easy way is to note the finch's location in the cage and turn off the lights, then reach inside and grasp it gently. In a larger aviary, you'll probably need to purchase a finch net (which is made of very fine mesh) to catch your birds.

Wing clipping: A definite no-no

A common practice with many larger companion birds is to clip the primary flight feathers to make flying more difficult for the bird. This is often necessary during taming, and many people choose to clip the bird's flight feathers throughout the bird's life.

Do not clip your finches' flight feathers! Finches fly for their exercise. They don't climb like parrots, and they're rarely finger-tamed. Their one and only true exercise is flight. If you prevent your finches from flying, their health will suffer in very short order.

The only time anyone ever clips a finch's wing feathers is if a particularly aggressive male is in an aviary during breeding season. The bird keeper may choose to gently clip two of the flight feathers on each wing just to slow the bully down a bit — but not to prevent him from flying.

No matter how you catch your finch, you need to make sure you hold the bird correctly for toenail clipping. Your hand should surround the finch, snugly but without squeezing. Be certain that you don't cover your finch's *nares* (nostrils). Hold the finch in your left hand (or right hand, if you're left-handed), and secure the foot between your thumb and index finger, so that the foot doesn't wiggle during the procedure. Your finch will try to curl her feet close to her body. Your finger grip should be firm enough to prevent this without injuring your finch.

A finch's toenails are very small. Just like in other animals, a blood vessel extends nearly to the tip of the nail. This blood supply is called the *quick* (see Figure 5-2). Because of your finch's tiny size, a small mishap that would produce little more than a drop of blood from your cat or dog can be life threatening to your finch. Be sure to clip in a very well lighted place. If your finch has light-colored nails, you'll be able to see the quick of the nail (the blood supply). Do not cut into this! If the nails are dark, cut only the very tip. Be conservative.

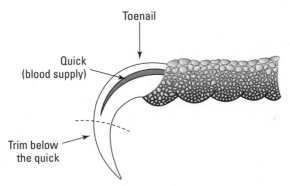

Figure 5-2: Do not cut into the quick when you trim your bird's nails.

Keep a supply of styptic powder on hand to stop bleeding if you do have a mishap with your bird. Don't try to apply the powder to the nail. Instead, gently insert the nail into a dish or container of the powder and wait for the bleeding to stop. If you wait for bleeding to stop naturally without using styptic powder, your bird may become weak or even die. A bar of soap works in an emergency, as does baking flour.

For a clipping tool, human nail clippers will work very well, if you use care in clipping. Clippers for human baby nails are great. Round nail clippers used to clip cat nails are good as well.

Never groom your finch's beak

Trimming a finch's beak is a very delicate procedure. Because a mistake could easily prevent your bird from eating, you need to be sure that beak-trimming is done by a veterinary professional (if it's necessary).

Problems with a finch's beak can occur from injury, mites, genetic problems, and malnutrition. A veterinarian should address any beak issues.

A cuttlebone does help to prevent problems. A finch, like any bird, will clean his beak on a rough perch or cuttlebone immediately after eating, which helps keep the beak from overgrowing. A cuttlebone has the added advantage of providing additional calcium for your bird's diet.

If you're in any doubt as to how to clip your finch's nails correctly, take him to the avian veterinarian. Your vet should be able to do a good and safe job of clipping your bird's toenails in his office and show you how to do it safely at home as well.

Bathing your bird

Finches love to bathe. Moisture is necessary for the health of your bird's feathers and skin. Provide a clean, shallow dish of room-temperature water (use filtered or bottled water, free of chlorine, and not more than ½ to ¾-inch deep), and change the water frequently. Your finches will dip their beaks in the water and even drink from it. They'll also splash about and flap their wings a lot, scattering water droplets as much as 10 feet from the cage. This is another good reason for situating your finches' cage over a floor that can be cleaned easily!

Make a clean bath available for your finches daily. Most finches will bathe several times a week at least. Remove and replace soiled water promptly.

In the rare event that you have a finch who seems suspicious of a bath, or who is reluctant to bathe for another reason, you can use a mister to spray her by hand. The spray should be very, very fine and gentle and always applied from above and behind your bird. Some birds simply love being sprayed with a mister and will raise their wings and turn this way and that under the light spray.

Be careful not to drench the cage or nest. And never spray your finch in the face.

Giving your molting bird some TLC

Molting refers to the process of feathers dropping off your bird and new ones growing in to replace them. Although loss of feathers at the wrong times can be a sign of stress or illness, molting is a perfectly normal process for any bird and does not indicate poor health.

When you see feathers at the bottom of the cage, it's probably just the result of normal molting. Take your bird to the vet if you see feathers at the bottom of his cage and if any of the following is true:

✔ Your finch stops eating.

✔ Your finch spends more than half the day sleeping.

✔ You see bald patches on the bird.

Molting usually happens when there are changes in light, such as the days growing longer in the springtime and shorter in the winter. Captive finches often molt several times in a single year.

Even though molting is completely natural, it does cause an unusual amount of stress for your bird, and he needs some additional care during these periods. When your finches begin to molt, they'll sleep more than usual. After a day or two, you'll begin to notice fallen feathers at the bottom of the cage. A few days into the molt, your finch will probably look a little scruffy and threadbare. This is normal. As the new feathers begin to grow in, the bird will spend an unusual amount of time preening, and you may think he's itching. Resist the temptation to treat for mites unless you're certain that your finch has a mite problem.

Additional calcium helps a great deal during the molting process. In addition, give your birds plenty of access to direct sunlight. Sunlight helps their bodies produce vitamins and hormones that help with the molting process. ***Remember:*** Make sure that they have a shaded area to retreat to — direct sunlight can become too warm for your finches very quickly. Let your birds decide how much or how little they need.

Your birds can breed during molt, but it isn't a great idea. If possible, prevent breeding by not providing nesting material for them. Both breeding and molting are very stressful periods for your birds — so why combine the two if you can avoid it?

As the molt continues, you'll notice *pin feathers* appearing all over your bird, giving the bird a spiky appearance. New feathers, called *pin feathers,* are covered in a hard, tight, keratin sheath so that they can break through the skin. The finches preen to pull these sheaths off the new feather growth. The sheaths will disintegrate into a fine dust on the bottom of your bird's cage and sometimes the floor surrounding it. This is also completely normal. Bathing will help the sheathes to become soft and easy to preen away.

(continued)

(continued)

> Molting periods vary widely among species. Sometimes the bird doesn't come out of molt at all. This situation is referred to as being *stuck in the molt,* and it's usually due to dietary or health problems. Consult your avian veterinarian in the event that this happens to any of your finches. You want to correct this situation as quickly as possible. If your finch is losing feathers and not growing new ones, his cage mates may harass him, and he may even lose the ability to fly.

Can't We All Just Get Along? Living with Other Pets

Finches are delicate, sensitive animals, and they won't "get along" with other pets. More likely, your other pets will want to eat or kill your finches. Dogs, cats, snakes, ferrets, rats, and other similar animals all pose a threat to your finches. Keep other pets away from your birds.

Although your goldfish won't leap from his bowl and kill your bird, his fish tank or bowl can pose a drowning threat to a finch that's allowed free flight in your home. A deep dog or cat water bowl can be dangerous as well.

Some finches can get along with some other species of birds if they are all given enough space, as in a very large aviary. For example, zebra finches, society finches, and Gouldian finches can all live together with cockatiels and budgies (parakeets). Even though these species *can* live together, you must always watch for squabbles and separate aggressive birds.

Larger parrots will not get along with finches.

Chapter 6

Come Here Often? Getting to Know Your Finch

In This Chapter

▶ Understanding what your finch is telling you

▶ Handling your finch without hurting him

▶ Increasing your finch population

*T*he finch is so popular because it's a bird that lets you into its world. Unlike parrots, finches generally don't become attached to people, so they just go about their business as they would in the wild, and because of this they are absolutely charming to watch. This chapter helps you recognize normal and abnormal finch behavior and gives you the basics of breeding.

Understanding Finch Behavior

If you've never lived with companion birds before, much of their behavior probably seems incomprehensible. Take heart: Your finches are not that difficult to understand. With a few simple pointers, you'll know your birds' needs with ease.

What did you say?: Normal finch vocalization

Finches are very social creatures, and social interaction within the flock requires a certain amount of noise. Zebra finches and most of the other Australian exotic finches have a fixed number of vocalizations broken into two categories — calls and songs:

- ✔ **Calls** are short vocalizations meant for communications. A contact call, for example, keeps immediate neighbors in a flock together. Another louder call serves to maintain contact between mates that are some distance from one another, or to keep an entire flock together. A different call signifies warning or aggression. Your finch's calls might just sound like "meep meep" or "wheet wheet" to you, but they actually mean something to another finch.

- ✔ **Songs** are longer and more complex than calls. The male sings to attract a mate, to keep her, and to get her into breeding condition. Females are biologically programmed to want to mate when they hear the male's song. The male also uses song to keep other males out of his territory. By singing, he lets them know he's there. Females rarely sing, though some individuals will sing a bit, but generally not the complex songs of the male.

By watching your birds, you'll come to understand what their vocalizations mean. For example, if you hear your male finch make a certain vocalization when he wants his mate to return to the nest, and he does this every time he wants her to return, you'll be able to recognize that vocalization when you're out of the room and know what your finches are doing. When the male is singing, you'll know that he's in breeding condition and he's trying to get the female ready as well.

Most of the sounds your finches will make will be soft chirps and tweeps — inoffensive to all but the most curmudgeonly human.

You scratch my back, I'll scratch yours: Preening and allopreening

Your finches probably spend a lot of time grooming, and you may wonder if they're just obsessed with their looks. Don't worry — they're not planning their big break in Hollywood. There's a real reason for what your birds are doing. This self-grooming is called *preening,* and it helps them to maintain the preen gland oil in their feathers and helps to keep them clean.

If you have two finches paired off, they'll groom one another — this is called *allopreeing.* One partner will sidle up to the other and turn to expose the part of his body he would like to have groomed; the other party will carefully draw a feather right through her beak.

Stretching: Birdy yoga

Finches stretch just like humans do and for the same reasons. They extend a wing, a leg, and sometimes both at the same time on the same side, which is called *mantling*. Males also stretch their necks when they sing.

Hungry anyone? Finch vomiting and regurgitation

Just like a human, a bird can vomit, which is a stressful and distressing behavior that is usually the result of illness, overheating, or poisoning. If a bird is vomiting, you'll notice him shaking his head to remove the vomit from his beak. You may see dried and crusted vomit around his beak and/or on his chest.

If you notice your bird vomiting, get him to the avian veterinarian right away.

However, if the bird is showing no other sign of illness, he's probably simply *regurgitating* — which means that he's bringing up partially-digested food from his crop (food that has never reached his gizzard and never been digested) to feed hatchlings or to feed a hen as a part of courting her or so that she can feed the nestlings herself. This behavior is a sign of affection, part of the breeding process, and completely normal.

Resting on one leg

A finch rests on one leg to conserve body warmth. The behavior is usually accompanied by somewhat fluffed-up feathers. It's merely part of the normal sleeping posture and only healthy birds show this behavior. Don't worry; the arrangements of muscle and tendon in a bird's leg won't let him come tumbling off his perch.

Scratching

Finches scratch during molting, which is an itchy time for a finch's skin. They also scratch when they have a regular old itch, just like humans do.

Scratching is sometimes an indication of feather mites in finches. If you notice your finch scratching a lot, and he isn't molting, take your finch to a veterinarian to get a firm diagnosis and then treat the condition if the doctor suspect mites.

Romeo, Romeo . . .: When your finch goes a-courting

Courting behavior differs among species of finches. Some fire-finches and waxbills will present the female with a long blade of grass, indicating a desire to build a nest. Others, including the zebra finch, sing to a prospective mate as well as bend down in front of her and brush his bill back and forth.

Finch Communication

Finches in the wild communicate using calls, songs, and body language. Finches in captivity do the same. Some finches are very social, like the zebra and the society finches, and they'll all want to eat, bathe, and nap at approximately the same time.

Communicating with your finch will probably be pretty basic. You can talk softly and soothingly to your finches, sing to them, make clicking noises, and whistle. You may or may not get a response from them. Each finch is different, and whether they respond to you has everything to do with how much human contact they had when they were young and how much they trust you.

Handling Your Finch Safely

There are very few reasons to handle your finches. You may need to clip long nails at times, or you may need to move the birds from one cage to another, or take them to the veterinarian, but these are pretty much the only reasons to handle your finches. If you have a tame finch, that's another story — but you probably won't.

If you simply want to move finches from one cage to another, you can use a net specifically made for birds. This net has a very fine mesh that the bird's nails can't get caught in, unlike a fish net that can easily catch a bird's toe.

Handling your finch

If you need to handle your finch for any reason, you can simply grasp the bird with your bare hand. You don't need gloves — your finch won't hurt you. A parrot's bite will hurt, but a finch's bite won't, and it's unlikely that a finch will try to bite anyway. He'll be too scared to do anything but squirm.

Grasp the bird firmly enough to keep it in your hand, but don't squeeze him. Constricting a bird around the chest will prevent him from breathing. Only hold the finch for as long as you need to complete the procedure. Finches can panic and even die if they're extremely frightened.

Children and finches

Very young or unruly children can be dangerous to your finches. But when a child is ready, he can learn a tremendous amount from finches about the natural world and how to care for small animals. A finch is certainly never a danger to a child — it's usually the other way around.

Curious children should be taught to enjoy finches at a safe distance. They can watch their little birds by the hour, but attempts to handle them should be restricted to a need-only basis and done only by an adult or older child. Your house rules must also be made extremely clear — even for kids who spend the night.

Here are some basic ground rules to share with your children when you first bring your finches home:

- ✔ **Move slowly.** Birds are frightened by quick movements. Explain to the child that the bird won't hurt him and that it's important to remain calm, no matter what happens.

- ✔ **Speak softly.** A screaming child is terrifying to finches. Instruct your child to use a soft, soothing voice when talking to his bird.

- ✔ **Don't stick fingers in the cage.** Teach your child not to stick his fingers or other objects into the cage. A child should not feed the finch without supervision, either, because the child may feed the bird something she shouldn't have.

✔ **Never shake, hit, or rattle the cage.** Finches are going to be only as entertaining as they can be. Your child may not understand this and may try to get the finch to do something more interesting. Explain to the child that the finch becomes frightened when his home is rattled.

✔ **Never take the finch outside.** Your child may want to show off her bird to friends, and though that's a valid response, many dangers lurk outside — including the bird flying away.

Dealing with Problem Behaviors

"Problem" behaviors in finches aren't like "problem" behaviors in parrots. With parrots, a problem behavior may be biting or screaming. You won't have these problems with finches. The problems that you may see involve behaviors that are signs of illness (see Chapter 7 for a list of behaviors that indicate illness).

Some finches get aggressive with their mates during breeding and nesting, so watch out for squabbles. Some finches, like the canary, don't like other birds in the cage with them when they aren't breeding, and they'll become aggressive. If you notice a finch picking on others, put him in a separate cage for a few days. When you put him back with the others, watch him closely.

Taming Your Finch

Unlike parrot-type birds, most people don't tame or train a finch. The best you'll probably get out of a finch is for her to tolerate your presence in the room, or perhaps she'll come to trust you enough to hop over to the side of the cage and take a worm from your hand. If you're a very patient person, you can try allowing your finches to fly in the bird-proofed room where their cage is, and you can sit nearby, quietly, holding a treat. Eventually the finches may come to you.

If you breed finches, you may have the opportunity to hand-raise a finch if the parents toss it out of the nest, abandon it, have too many babies to care for, or die. Hand-feeding finches isn't easy, but many people do accomplish it. Hand-feeding isn't without risks for your finches, so it's a good idea to get hands-on advice and help from a finch expert in your area who has successfully hand-fed finches before. Don't hand-feed finches just to have tame pets — many babies being hand-fed do not make it.

Breeding Your Finches

Breeding many finches is easy, but breeding them well and producing the best results is a little harder. Some species are very difficult to breed, and some of the more common species, such as zebras and society finches, will breed themselves to death if you let them. The following sections give you the basics on breeding finches if you choose to do so.

Making sure you have a male and a female

This may sound like a no-brainer, but you have to start with a male and a female. Some finches — including zebras, Gouldians, and olive finches — are *dimorphic,* meaning that you can tell the males from the females. Other finches — including society finches, red-headed parrot finches, and canaries — are *monomorphic,* and you won't be able to tell the difference between the sexes by looking at them.

How can you determine which bird is male and which is female? That varies from species to species. If you purchase your finches from a breeder, he'll tell you ways to determine the sex of your finches. But here are a few examples:

- ✔ **Zebra finches:** As in many bird species, the male is more spectacular in color and patterning. He has a reddish-orange beak, as opposed to the yellowish beak of the female. He has bright patches on either side of his head, usually orange in color. He also has pronounced black and white bars on his chest, which the female doesn't have. ***Remember:*** This is a description of the *typical* zebra finch. Different color mutations do exist.

- ✔ **Society finches:** You won't be able to tell the difference between a male and a female society finch by looking at it. The best way to tell with a society finch is to listen for singing — only the male will sing.

- ✔ **Gouldian finches:** The males have a brighter chest. A male has a vivid head color that is duller in the female. In general, the male is more vivid and the female is more muted. Also, males sing and females do not.

- ✔ **Whydahs:** During breeding season, the male grows a spectacular tail that is often twice the length of his body.

✔ **Owl finches:** The male's breast band is thicker than the female's, and the area of white on his face is larger.

✔ **Canaries:** Only the male sings. Sometimes females can have a rudimentary song, but it won't be as developed as the male's.

✔ **Weavers:** The male is bright and colorful in breeding season. Outside of breeding season, he looks like a female. If you get weaver finches when the male isn't in full color, watch the birds carefully — the male weaves a nest but the female doesn't.

✔ **Spice finches:** You can't tell the difference between the male and female by looking at these birds. However, the male sings a soft song and does a courtship dance to the female.

When you choose your breeding pair, make sure they get along and that they're a true pair. Watch for one bird bullying the other, quibbling between the birds, or an obvious lack of preference for each other's company. If they spend time together, share food, groom each other, and prefer to bed down together for the night, the chances are excellent that you've chosen a compatible pair.

Starting with healthy birds

If you've decided to breed, your first priority is to ensure that your birds are in the best health possible. Don't breed while your birds are molting or ill, because this already places them under considerable stress. Look for brilliant, healthy feathers, bright eyes, and a perky disposition. Having your veterinarian check them over before breeding is a good idea, but it isn't an absolute requirement.

Make certain that the pair you choose to breed are not related. If you bought them from a breeder, he should be able to assure you of this. If you buy your birds from a pet store, you won't have any way of knowing, and the chances are that your pet store doesn't know for certain either.

Though most finches can breed as early as 3 months, do not allow them to breed until they are from 6 to 9 months of age. Some breeders recommend waiting a full year. Breeding puts a tremendous amount of stress on the parents.

Knowing when to breed

Finches in the wild will breed whenever the conditions are right. They breed when they can find sufficient quantities of water and the foods they need to produce healthy offspring and remain healthy themselves. Captive finches breed year-round, because food, water, and a safe environment are always there for them.

Constant breeding poses a health threat to your finches, so don't allow them to breed more than about three times per year.

Getting the right equipment

If your breeding finches are in a cage with several pairs of birds, you may have fights on your hands, depending on the species. Society finches, zebras, and Gouldians are usually fairly peaceful in an aviary together as long as they have enough space.

In terms of nests, most finches prefer an enclosed nest, though canaries prefer a wicker-cup nest. Bamboo finch nests are very popular, cheap, and easy to find (see Figure 6-1). You may also be able to find a grass and twig type of nest, or a wooden box, which will work for Gouldians. Many types of nests are available, from hollow gourds to clay pots. Weaver finches prefer to weave elaborate nests of their own. Check into the needs of your species before you choose a nest.

Your breeding finches will also need a quantity of soft material to line their nest. You can buy commercial nesting material, but coming up with materials yourself is often more fun. Some ideas include shredded burlap, clean pet fur, dried grass, molted feathers, pine needles, coconut fiber, dried moss, and cotton pads.

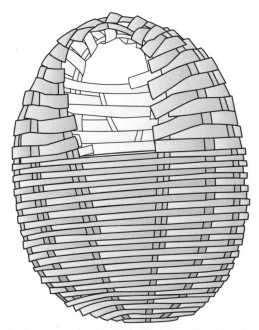

Figure 6-1: Bamboo nests like this one are popular with finches.

Make sure that any nesting materials you use aren't long enough to get wrapped around a little toe, leg, or neck. Also, bamboo nests can sometimes catch a little toe in the spaces between the weaves, so make sure that both of your finches can leave the nest every day.

Figuring out where to put the nest

Place the nest inside the cage as high as possible and in a corner. If you're using a wooden box, you can hang the box on the outside of the cage. Only put the next outside of the cage if your home is free of hazards, particularly from small children or other pets. The last thing you want to do is have your finches frightened away from their nest.

Knowing what the parents need to eat

A breeding finch's diet needs protein, either from hard-boiled eggs or live insects, offered daily. Egg food is also great for nesting finches, as well as for their chicks. Calcium is also extremely important for breeding hens.

None of the foods you feed your finches should change during breeding, but the amounts — especially of calcium and proteins — should be boosted. Start to condition your birds for breeding months before you add the nest. Bulking them up before they breed is a great way of ensuring that the chicks will be healthy and the hen won't have problems laying her eggs and rearing her babies.

Understanding the incubation period

Finches normally share the incubation period, with both the male and the female taking turns sitting in the nest and keeping the eggs warm. Because most finch nests have a cover, telling when your hen starts to lay may be difficult.

Typically, the hen will lay one egg per day until she's finished. Finches average between one and six eggs in a *clutch* (a group of babies). The hen will become more and more reluctant to leave the nest, but the male will spend part of the day incubating the eggs and give her a break for food and movement. She will also bathe and bring the moisture back to her eggs.

The incubation period for finches ranges from 12 days for some of the waxbills, to 13 days for zebras, to 15 days for Gouldians. If you can, peek inside the nest when the parents are out of it. Leave them alone as much as possible, but try to peek at least once a day after she's done laying all the eggs. If a week goes by and the eggs don't change color a little — usually turning grayish or growing darker — chances are that the eggs aren't fertile.

If you want to know for sure if the eggs are fertile, you can buy a *candler*, which is a little flashlight with a long wand at the end. Place the end of the wand gently on the egg and you'll see veins and the outline of an embryo if one exists. This is called *candling* the egg, and it's a common practice among breeders.

Don't panic if you can't see the eggs at first glance. Finches commonly cover the eggs with a bit of nesting material to help keep them warm. However, if they bury the eggs too deeply, the chicks will die when they hatch. This is why keeping an eye on the nest is a good idea.

Occasionally, you'll have fertile eggs that don't hatch. Often, the parents leave the nest for too long and allow the eggs to become cold. If they're nervous, they may stay out of the nest. It's important for the parent finches to have peace and quiet during this period. Disturb them only to supply them with food and water.

The eggs will hatch one per day, in the order in which they were laid. The hatchlings don't look much like birds at all (see Figure 6-2). A few species have little bits of fluff on them, but they don't really have down yet. If you look closely at them, you'll actually be able to see food in their crops if the parents are feeding them. Making sure right away that they're being fed is important (see the following section for more information).

Figure 6-2: Don't be alarmed — hatchlings don't really resemble adult birds.

Helping your finch survive the loss of a mate

Although finches are not always monogamous, they do prefer to pair with another finch for life. When one of two paired birds dies, from illness or any other cause, this is terribly stressful for the survivor. If the mate's death was not due to illness, you may want to introduce another bird as a companion right away. Place the new finch in a cage next to the old one, and allow them to get to know each other for a few days. If they seem to get along, you can add the old finch to the new finch's cage.

If the hen died during incubating or rearing chicks, foster or hand-feed the chicks right away. Sometimes, the male will take up rearing duties. Keep an eye on the babies to make sure they're being fed.

Knowing what to do when something goes wrong

A number of things can go wrong when your birds breed. The first problem, which is the most minor as well as the most obvious, is that your breeding pair may not like each other. In that case, it's back to the drawing board. Rearrange your birds and try again.

The next most likely thing to go wrong is *egg binding,* which is when the female cannot pass her egg. Symptoms include a midsection that stays swollen more than a day, as well as a general listlessness and puffed-up appearance. Chapter 7 provides more information on what to do if your finch suffers from egg binding. If your hen survives, don't breed her again until she is fully recovered and you've boosted her calcium and nutrient intake.

The first eggs that your hen lays may not be fertile — not a major problem. Wait 21 days to be certain that the eggs won't hatch, and then remove the eggs. You can leave the nest and nesting material intact. Your hen should begin laying again immediately. If you don't want her to lay again, simply remove the nest.

Some parents don't feed their first clutch, but they usually get the idea by the second clutch. If you notice that the parents aren't feeding their babies, you can foster them under society finches that also have babies (put them in the society's nest), or finches of the same species that have proved themselves to be good parents. If you can't do this, you can try to hand-feed them yourself.

Many people are frightened because the crop on a brand new hatchling appears grotesquely swollen with food. This is not a problem. It means that your finches are feeding the hatchlings and feeding them well. If the crop becomes too full, the hatchling cannot raise her head and ask for more until it goes down a bit — she won't explode, despite appearances.

In the early days, of your hatchlings lives, you need to ensure that the parents are still fed as well as they were in the days leading up to the hatching. Remember that the male finch may be eating for as many as eight mouths (sometimes including the hen). So even if he's the only one you see eating, keep the groceries coming.

Tossing is a particularly ugly problem. Once in a while, one of the parents simply tosses a chick out of the nest. Gouldians do this often, but any species will exhibit the behavior now and then. Some of the possible causes include a finch that simply doesn't know what to do with a wiggling baby or parents rattled by too much or too intrusive checking of the nest. You may just have a bird that habitually tosses the babies out of the nest. The only solution to this is fostering the chicks with another set of parents (see the following section).

In some cases, chicks don't thrive. They lose weight and die before reaching adulthood. In many cases, this is due to inbreeding, so be sure not to breed that particular pair again. Now and then, a bacterial or fungal infection too mild to trouble the adults can cause death for the chicks. The only person who can determine this is your veterinarian. Have the doctor examine the body of any chick who doesn't make it.

If your chicks survive the first three days, they'll probably make it.

Finding foster parents for your babies

Zebra finches and society finches are very good foster parents. The foster parents don't need to be of the same species as the hatchlings, although feeding the foster parents a diet close to the natural diet of the fostered chicks is a good idea. Contrary to the myths surrounding fostering, the babies will grow up to be full-fledged members of their own species, and they won't exhibit the behaviors of their foster parents when they grow to adulthood.

Choose a species known for successful fostering. Society finches seem to be the best foster parents, with zebras running a close second. Choose foster parents that have unflappable temperaments. If you're fostering eggs that have been abandoned, be certain that the foster parents don't see you add the eggs to their nest. Fostering is always a throw of the dice, but it's well worth the effort.

Oh, give me a home . . .: Finding good homes for your baby finches

Finding homes for your baby finches could prove to be your biggest problem. Letting the little ones go can be very difficult.

If you take your baby finches to a pet shop, there is a chance that they won't go to good homes. In fact, some people *feed* cheap finches to their larger birds, like toucans.

Giving them away may help you find the most homes in the shortest period, but try to sell them for a reasonable price if you can. When you charge a fair price for your finches, you may be more likely to find people who take the responsibility seriously.

Chapter 7

Keeping Your Finch Healthy and Handling Emergencies

*P*art of taking care of your feathered friend is making sure he's healthy and getting him help when he's not. In this chapter, I help you find a vet for your bird, figure out when you should go, and identify the different signs and symptoms of some finch illnesses.

The Veterinarian: Your New Best Friend

For your finch, you want an *avian veterinarian,* a vet who specializes in the care and treatment of birds. The best place to find an avian vet in your area is by calling the Association of Avian Veterinarians at 561-393-8901 or by visiting www.aav.org.

Regular examinations

Your birds should have regular examinations to ensure optimum health and prevent problems before they become serious. Ask your veterinarian what an appropriate schedule for your birds should be.

Take your new pet to an avian veterinarian within three days of buying him. Here's why:

- ✔ If you bought your finch with a health guarantee, you'll have some recourse if tests reveal that your new bird is ill.

- ✔ You'll begin a relationship with the vet, and the vet will get to know your bird and be able to evaluate him better because the doctor will know what your bird is like when he's healthy.

- ✔ Some avian vets won't take an emergency patient unless the bird is a regular client. You don't want to be stuck without someone to call if your finch encounters an emergency.

- ✔ Avian vets often board birds in their offices, though some will only board clients — that way they can be relatively sure that the bird won't bring diseases into their office.

- ✔ You'll get some important recommendations from the doctor, including information on diet and housing.

Even when your finches are well, you should take them to your avian veterinarian at least once a year. Your veterinarian will run some routine tests and weigh your birds. This *well-bird check-up* will allow your veterinarian to keep records of your healthy bird and will make it easier to determine when he's ill.

Emergencies

When you have an emergency involving your finch, you *must* take him to an avian veterinarian right away. So what qualifies as an emergency?

If you have *one single moment* of worry about something that has happened to your bird (he's flown into a window, broken a toe, is bleeding, and so on), or if you notice a drastic change in your finch's behavior, you probably have an emergency.

Don't hesitate to rush your bird to the avian veterinarian. Minutes are crucial in an emergency. ***Remember:*** Your bird is a small, sensitive creature more likely to be overcome by the stress of an accident than a larger animal.

What a Healthy Finch Looks Like

Knowing something about the finch's bodily systems and observing your bird carefully when he's healthy will help you to be able to tell if he's ill.

Eyes

A healthy eye is clear, moist, and free of discharge. A finch with an eye problem may squint or scratch it excessively with his foot, or he'll rub his eye on the perch or sides of his cage.

If you see swollen eyelids, cloudy eyes, excessive blinking or discharge, and tearing, have your bird checked out by your vet.

Ears

Your finch's ears are located a short distance parallel from the eyes and look like holes in the head. Each ear opening is covered by feathers. You may get a glimpse of the ear openings after your finch bathes, when the feathers around his head are wet and stuck together.

If you can see your finch's ear opening without the bird being wet, make an appointment with your avian veterinarian.

Beak

Your finch's beak is made of the same durable material as your fingernails. The beak grows over a basically hollow honeycomb-like structure, a convenient design for an animal that should be light enough to fly. The beak acts as a crushing tool but is delicate enough to peel the skin off a pea.

Your finch should be able to keep his beak trim through eating and playing. If your bird's beak is overgrown, it could be an indication of a nutritional disorder or mites, and you'll have to take him to an avian veterinarian for treatment.

Never try to trim your finch's beak yourself.

Feet

In addition to walking and grasping, birds also use their feet to regulate their body temperature. When your finch is cold, he may draw one leg up into his body and stand on the other leg. When your finch is warm, the blood flow will increase to his legs, which will help his whole body cool down.

Several injuries are common to the feet, including catching toes on cages and toys, as well as problems with the leg band. Swelling in the legs could be a symptom of *gout* (a painful condition that can be the result of poor nutrition). If the skin on the bottom of the foot is red and inflamed, or even scabby, this could be a sign of *bumblefoot* (an infection associated with poor nutrition and obesity).

 If you notice something wrong with your bird's legs or feet, take him to your avian vet. Contact your avian veterinarian right away if you notice any foot or leg weakness or *lameness* (inability to walk).

Feathers

A healthy finch should be obsessed with taking care of his feathers, preening them for much of the day. A finch likes to keep his feathers neat, clean, and well organized on his body.

Birds *molt* (shed their feathers and grow new ones) once or twice a year, usually during seasonal changes. When your finch molts, you'll notice feathers on the bottom of the cage, but you shouldn't be able to see patches of skin on your bird. (If you do notice bald spots, contact your vet — it could indicate a serious medical problem.) When a new feather begins growing, it will be encased in a protective sheath called a *pin feather*. Pin feathers can be itchy and your finch may become cranky at this time, not wanting to be played with as often.

Respiratory system

Finches have a very sensitive respiratory system, which is sensitive to airborne irritants, such as aerosol sprays, fumes from heated nonstick cookware, and tobacco smoke. They're prone to respiratory illness and distress.

 If you notice your finch panting, call your avian veterinarian and describe the situation. Keep your finch away from fumes and airborne toxins.

 If you notice a change in your bird's breathing or, in extreme cases, bubbling from the mouth or nostrils, take your finch to the veterinarian right away. Your finch could have a respiratory infection.

Skeletal system

Many of your finch's bones are filled with air, and all of them are thin-walled, which makes them light enough for flight. Though bird bones are strong enough to allow the movement of wings in flight, they're easily broken.

 If you suspect that one of your finch's bones is broken, take him to the veterinarian immediately. Some of the bones contain air sacs that aid in breathing, and your bird may experience respiratory problems if he has broken bones. Symptoms should be relatively obvious — if you see your bird with a leg or wing hanging, or if the bird goes lame, it could indicate a break. Of course, if you see a break (as you would in a human), you'll know right away.

Digestive system

The finch's digestive system begins with the beak and ends with the vent. After your bird swallows food, the food goes to the *crop* near the bird's breast. From the crop, the food goes to the stomach then on to the *gizzard,* which grinds the food. Then the food moves on to the *cloaca,* where the feces, *urates* (the off-white or yellowish part of the dropping), and urine collect before being eliminated through the *vent.*

Because your finch will probably be munching all day, she'll be pooping all day too. This is normal. Frequent elimination is a function of flying — a bird that's holding a load of waste is going to be heavier, so nature gave birds a smaller area to hold that waste, so it has to be eliminated often.

Waste should have three parts to it — a green solid-ish part, a yellowish white part (urates), and a watery part (urine). Sometimes the color of the waste changes according to what you're feeding your bird. If you feed blueberries or beets, for example, expect the color to change. If you feed greens, expect there to be more urine in the feces — this is normal and isn't considered diarrhea. If you notice a drastic change in your bird's droppings, see your avian veterinarian.

 One common digestive disorder comes from feeding grit to finches. Finches don't need grit the way other types of bird may. If your finch eats too much grit, it can stay in the crop and cause impaction. The crop won't be able to empty and will become distended. You may notice bloody feces with undigested seeds in it.

Signs and Symptoms of Sick Finches

An ill finch will sit very quietly in the cage and may sleep a good deal. Sleeping a lot in the daytime is a fairly obvious sign of trouble. In addition, your bird will puff up his feathers, attempting to control his body temperature and stay warm.

There are other signs that may indicate a variety of problems. Respiratory distress (panting), bleeding, a wet and messy vent, or failure to eat, especially if the food offered is of a type your finch has enjoyed previously, can all be symptoms of illness.

Finches often lose weight rapidly. This is due to a variety of illnesses and should be addressed immediately.

 Place a sick finch in a separate, hospital cage as quickly as possible to avoid infecting other healthy birds (see "Assembling a First-Aid Kit" later in this chapter). As soon as possible, take your finch to your avian veterinarian.

Any odd behavior may indicate illness but not always. Finches, like most birds, are creatures of routine, and a sudden break in routine signals that you should investigate your bird's condition.

 If you can't find any reason for the unusual behavior, start looking for symptoms of illness, including the following:

- ✔ **Fluffiness:** If you notice that your finch is overly fluffy, he may be trying to retain heat.

- ✔ **Sleepiness:** A sick finch may sleep too much. Sleeping on the bottom of the cage is especially telling.

- ✔ **Loss of appetite:** If you notice that your bird isn't eating, he could have a serious problem.

- ✔ **Weight loss:** Weight loss is a sign of a number of illnesses. *Mycobacterium avium* is responsible for the tuberculosis infection and can be transmitted in food, water, or by filthy cage parts. It can be transmitted to humans with compromised immune systems, so be careful to avoid infection.

- ✔ **Change in attitude:** If your finch is not behaving in his usual manner, he may be ill.

✔ **Change in feathers:** Lack of grooming and feathers falling out in patches can indicate illness, as can abnormal feather growth. If you notice a change in your bird's feathers, take him to see your avian vet.

✔ **Lameness:** If your bird can't use his feet, you can be guaranteed that something is wrong.

✔ **Panting or labored breathing:** Either of these symptoms can indicate a respiratory ailment, or perhaps overheating. Changes in your finch's breathing, changes in vocalization, or gasping or wheezing can be a sign of infection. Be sure to take your finch to the avian vet right away if you notice respiratory problems.

✔ **Tail bobbing:** If your finch is standing straight up on the perch and his tail is noticeably bobbing toward and away from him, he may have a respiratory problem, or he may just be out of breath.

✔ **Listlessness:** A formerly active finch who has become listless and uninterested in life may be ill.

✔ **Discharge:** If you notice any runniness or discharge on the eyes, nostrils, or vent, go to the veterinarian immediately.

✔ **Food stuck to the feathers around the face:** This indicates poor grooming or vomiting — possible signs of illness.

✔ **Sticky substance in mouth or white mouth lesions:** These can be signs of a yeast infection, which can affect the mouth and digestive tract, and can involve the respiratory system. Your finch normally has a certain amount of yeast in its body, but when his bodily balance is out a whack, when he is under-nourished or after a treatment of antibiotics, the fungus can grow to excess. Regurgitation and digestive problems may occur. Treatment by a veterinarian is necessary. Even though this condition is not immediately serious, it can cause death if left untreated.

✔ **Swollen abdomen:** A swollen abdomen could indicate egg binding in a female finch (see Chapter 6 for more information). Consult your veterinarian immediately if you suspect this problem. Normally, an egg is passed within a day of noticeable swelling. Even if she does pass the egg, take her to the veterinarian as soon as you can.

✔ **Drastic change in droppings:** Your finch's droppings should consist of a solid green portion, white urates (on top of the green), and a clear liquid. If any of these are discolored (darker green, black, yellow, or red) and there has been *no change in diet,* your bird may have a problem.

✔ **Clicking sound when breathing:** This is a symptom of air-sac mites, which is potentially deadly. Mites infest the respiratory system and respiratory distress occurs, followed by death. Products are available to kill these mites, but unfortunately, if your finch is heavily infested, the dead mites may asphyxiate the bird, and you can't do anything to save him. For this reason, many experts recommend treatment for air sac mites three to four times per year even if no symptoms are present.

✔ **Scratching:** This is a sign of feather mites or lice, which are rarely dangerous, except when the infestation is extremely severe. Even though they're usually not dangerous, they *are* miserable for your finch. See your vet if you notice your finch scratching.

Emergencies: Knowing When to Get Help Immediately

The average home offers plenty of dangers for finches. Even the most careful of keepers may encounter an accident with her birds.

When an accident happens, the first thing to do is contact your avian veterinarian. *Never* underestimate an emergency. If you notice weakness, a fluffed appearance, quick breathing, droopy eyes, the inability to perch, or your bird lying on the floor of the cage, rush your finch to the veterinarian right away.

In the following sections, I cover the more common emergencies. *Remember:* This list doesn't include everything that could happen to your bird, so if you notice something that doesn't seem quite right, don't be afraid to take your bird to the vet and have him checked out.

Poisoning

Poisoning generally happens when a finch gets into a household product. Ingestion or breathing in the poison are the most common ways a finch can become poisoned. Aerosol sprays and other products that leave a fine mist in the air can be particularly harmful for your little bird. Scented candles and plug-in air fresheners may seem harmless, but they can actually cause your finch respiratory distress. Even candle "beads" that are unlit can seem like neat pellets to your finch — and they can be deadly when ingested. Things like fertilizers, cleansers, and toxic houseplants are deadly, too. Keep your bird away from *all* household products.

Symptoms of poisoning can include vomiting, paralysis, bleeding from the eyes, nose, mouth, or vent, seizures, and shock.

 If you suspect that your bird has been poisoned, call the Animal Poison Control Center 24-hour poison hotline at 888-426-4435 (to pay by credit card) or 900-680-0000 (to have the charge automatically added to your phone bill). Rushing to your avian veterinarian is essential to saving your bird's life, though quick response from you with the help of the Animal Poison Control Center can be crucial.

Animal bites

Animals of all kinds, including your friendly cat, are a danger to finches.

 When a dog or a cat bites a finch, the wound, no matter how small, can be deadly in a matter of hours, or even minutes. Other animals have bacteria in their mouths that can cause a deadly infection in a bird.

 Even if your other pet was "just playing" with the bird, you should rush to the avian veterinarian right away. In the minutes before you take your bird to the veterinarian, flush a small wound, if you see one, with ⅔ water and ⅓ hydrogen peroxide. If the wound is large, leave it alone and let your veterinarian take care of it.

Overheating

 If your finch is panting, holding his wings out, standing on two feet, or is even lying on the floor of the cage, he may be overcome with heat.

 Keep a spray bottle handy and lightly mist your finch with cool water, repeating until he's soaked. Watch him closely until his behavior seems normal again. Make sure that he has cool water to drink at all times.

 Finches should never be kept in full sunlight unless they have a shady spot to retreat to.

If your bird does not respond to misting, remove him from the spot immediately and place him in a cooler environment. If you have a small fan, place the flow of air so that it hits just beside the cage, not directly on it, and mist him again. Put drops of cool water in his beak if he's unable to drink. Call your avian veterinarian.

Oil on the feathers

Oil on the feathers makes it difficult for a finch to regulate his body temperature, which can be deadly for a bird. The finch may also preen his feathers and ingest this oil, leading to medical problems. How does a finch get oil on his feathers? Believe it or not, finches occasionally fly into a pot of oil (cool oil, you hope!), or may even find themselves in the middle of an oily salad.

If your bird soaks himself in oil and is otherwise uninjured (the oil was cool), dust him with cornstarch or flour (any kind except gritty corn flour), making sure to keep the flour away from his face. Remove the excess flour with a paper towel. Fill a small bowl with warm water and add some grease-fighting liquid dish soap. Gently place the bird in the tub and allow him to soak. You may have to repeat this a few times. Do not scrub! Rinse him using the same method (without the soap), blot him dry, and place him in a hospital cage with a heating pad underneath half of it and most of the top covered. Don't restrict the flow of air, but keep the heat in. Use a thermometer and make sure the cage is between 80° and 90° F (26° and 32° C). Then get him to your avian veterinarian.

Frostbite

Frostbite can cause the loss of toes and feet and may even result in death. If you keep your finch outdoors during the cold season, consider bringing him inside as a preventative on the coldest nights. A finch will hold a frostbitten foot as if it were fractured (frostbite is a painful condition). The frostbitten area will die and turn a dark color.

If you find the condition early, place your bird in a hospital cage with a 90° F (32° C) temperature and call the veterinarian. If you catch the condition at the point where the affected area has already turned dark, get your bird to the avian veterinarian right away.

Unconsciousness

A bird may be unconscious for many reasons, but one strong possibility is that something is poisoning the air. If you find your bird unconscious, ventilate the room thoroughly and remove the bird from the area. Call your avian veterinarian immediately. If you're sure that there is no problem in the air, you can try to rouse your finch by gently handling him and trying to wake him. Get to your avian veterinarian right away.

Egg binding

A swollen abdomen may be a sign of egg binding in a female finch. If a hen is not well nourished, especially if she hasn't gotten enough calcium in her diet, her eggs may have soft shells, which will make the eggs difficult to lay, resulting in egg binding. Egg binding can also occur when the egg is malformed, or when the bird has a tumor or other disorder of the reproductive system. Symptoms of egg binding include panting and lameness. Consult your veterinarian immediately if you suspect this problem.

Normally, an egg is passed within a day of noticeable swelling. If you notice that your hen is having serious troubles and it's the middle of the night or you can't get to your avian veterinarian right away, move her to a warm (85° F to 90° F, or 29° C to 32° C) and humid hospital cage (see "Assembling a First-Aid Kit" later in this chapter, for tips on making such a cage). Put a few drops of mineral oil or olive oil in her beak with an eye dropper and place a few drops of the same in her vent (where the egg comes out). This may help her to pass the egg.

Even if she does pass the egg, take her to the veterinarian as soon as you can.

Foot injuries

Don't try to correct a serious foot injury. Place the injured bird in a hospital cage and take him to the vet immediately.

Eye injuries

If your finch's eye has come in contact with an irritant or poison, wash the eye out with saline solution before you take him to the veterinarian. If the injury is from a bite or other type of wound, place the bird in hospital cage until you can get to the veterinarian.

Seizures

A bird having seizures is in serious condition. Place him in a hospital cage and get to the veterinarian right away. If he comes out of the seizure, you may want to give him a few drops of sugar water to put some electrolytes and sugars into his bloodstream.

Injury to the beak

Often injuries to the beak can be fixed by a veterinarian, or the beak will heal itself by growing back. If your finch has injured his beak, place the bird in a hospital cage and take him to see the vet.

Fractures

Do not try to set a fracture by yourself. If you suspect a fracture, get your finch to the veterinarian right away. A serious break can lead to serious complications, especially if it occurs in one of the bones containing an air sac.

What to Do if Your Bird Is Lost

When you first get your finch, take a good photo of your bird to paste on signs and to post on the Internet in case he ever flies away. Tape his vocalizations and keep the tape handy — it may lure him down from the treetops when you play it back to him.

If your bird has already flown the coop, here's what to do:

- **Watch which way your finch is flying.** Try to keep him in sight as long as you can.

- **If he has a friend, bring the cage outside and let the two finches talk.** When your bird lands on the cage or comes nearer, approach slowly, talking softly, with a piece of millet in your hand.

- **Bring all your bird's favorite foods outside and tempt him with them.** Millet spray works well for this.

- **Bring his cage outside and fill it with his favorite foods and lots of water.** He may come down and enter his cage when he gets hungry.

- **If your finch hasn't come down by nightfall, but you have an idea of where he is, you can climb up to where he is and catch him.** A large bird net is really helpful for this. Birds don't see well in the dark and are easier to catch at night than they are in daylight.

✔ **If you don't catch your bird by the first evening, keep trying the tape of the vocalizations and tempting him with food.**

✔ **Make signs for your lost finch.** Place his photo on the sign, or clip out a picture of a similar looking finch from a book. Place signs within a two-mile radius — finches can fly long distances and you'll want to cover a large area.

✔ **Call your local bird club and pet shops and tell them about your lost bird in case someone contacts them about a bird she's found.**

Because finches aren't tame, your finch probably won't come back on his own. But it is likely that someone will find him, so don't lose hope.

Assembling a First-Aid Kit

The first and most important item in your finch first-aid kit is a well-set-up hospital cage or brooder, with a source of heat and humidity and a way to control them. Any sick, injured, or stressed bird is going to have trouble regulating its body temperature. It needs warmth, a way to slow down dehydration (humidity), and peace and quiet.

Making a hospital cage is easy. You'll need a 10 gallon aquarium, an aquarium thermometer, a heating pad, a screen top for the aquarium, paper towels, and a towel. Put the heating pad on the medium setting and place it underneath one half of the aquarium. Place a few layers of paper towels on the bottom of the aquarium. Make sure to put shallow dishes of food and water in the aquarium too — make sure the water is very shallow, because a weak bird can drown in water as deep as 2 inches. Place the bird in the aquarium; then cover the aquarium with the screen top. Cover the aquarium three-fourths of the way with a dark towel. The bird should be able to move away from the heat if she wants to. Make sure that the temperature in the tank stays at about 98° F to 99° F (about 37° C).

You may be in the position to treat a very minor injury yourself, or at least get it under control before you take your bird to your avian veterinarian.

Even though you'll be well equipped with your first-aid kit, it can't take the place of care by your avian veterinarian.

Your birdy first-aid kit should include:

- Alcohol (for cleaning your tools)
- Antibiotic ointment (a non-greasy kind, for dressing small wounds)
- Baby bird formula (for feeding babies or weak adults)
- Bandages and gauze (for dressing small wounds)
- Bottled water (for cleaning eyes or wounds)
- Cotton balls (for cleaning small wounds)
- Dishwashing detergent (mild, for cleaning tools)
- Eyedropper (for feeding weak birds)
- Eye wash (for rinsing eyes)
- Heating pad (for hospital cage)
- Hydrogen peroxide (for cleaning small wounds)
- Nail clippers (for clipping nails)
- Nail file (for filing nails)
- Pedialyte (to give to weak adult birds)
- Penlight (to see better)
- Q-Tips (for cleaning small wounds)
- Saline solution (for rinsing small wounds or eyes)
- Sanitary wipes (for your hands)
- Spray bottle (for spraying solutions onto wounds or eyes)
- Bird-safe styptic powder (to stop bleeding)
- Syringe (without needle, for feeding weak birds)
- Towels (small, to hold bird)
- Transport cage (to go to the veterinarian)
- Tweezers (for whatever comes up)
- Veterinarian's phone number (so you can call in an emergency)

Never give your finch any over-the-counter medication meant for humans or other animals. Instead of trying to remedy the bird yourself, take him to an avian veterinarian immediately.

For injuries and various illnesses, consider a few key items: *hemostats* (tools used to stop the flow of blood), surgical scissors, cotton swabs and bandage materials, nail clippers, Betadyne, Environclens (for disinfecting tools and cages), styptic powder (to stop bleeding), Calcivet (a calcium supplement for emergency treatment of egg binding), and any other drugs that your veterinarian recommends you keep on hand.

Ten Great Finch Web Sites

✔ **Zebra Finch Society:** `www.zebrafinch-society.org`
This site has helpful information about zebra finches and their care. You'll find photos, zebra finch mutation abbreviations, and informative articles.

✔ **National Finch and Softbill Society:** `www.nfss.org`
Founded in 1984, the National Finch and Softbill Society is devoted to all types of finches. Here you'll find dozens of articles on finch care and breeding, as well as a section for photos of members' birds.

✔ **HotSpot for Birds:** `www.multiscope.com/hotspot`
This site offers many articles about all types of birds, including finches, and contains a great deal of information about bird safety. It sells products as well.

✔ **ZBirds:** `www.zbirds.com`
This site specializes in all the mutations of zebra finches, including rare colors. It also has information about zebra finch pedigree software.

✔ **The Finch Niche:** `www.finchniche.com/index.mgi`
This is a very extensive site about all kinds of finches, finch care, safety, and mutations. The owner of the site is a passionate finch expert.

✔ **Finchworld:** `www.finchworld.com`
This site offers tons of great information on finches, especially about different species and types of finches. It has great photos as well.

✔ **EFinch:** `www.efinch.com/index.htm`
This site has lots of detailed finch information. You'll find excellent photos and detailed descriptions of finch species.

✔ **Zebra Finches on the Internet:** `http://zebrafinch.info`
This is a great hobby site with lots of information on mutations. It has a very cool "zebra finch designer," allowing you to interactively explore which zebra finch breedings would result in specific mutations.

✔ **Gouldian Finches Online:** `www.gouldianfinchesonline.com`
This site offers basic information on everything you'd need to care for and breed Gouldians.

✔ **Robirda Online:** `http://www.robirda.com/`
This site has extremely extensive information on canaries. It offers a newsletter, photos, membership, and a message board; the owner of the site will answer questions for a small fee.

Ten Ways to Prompt Your Finches to Breed

✔ **Separate the male and female into separate cages within close proximity of each other.**
Do this for about a week, and they should become so hot for each other that they'll breed soon after you reunite them.

✔ **Feed lots of protein, like crushed hard-boiled egg (including the shell) and mini-mealworms.**
The added protein will tell them that it's a time of "abundance," and they should be prompted to breed. The extra protein will put them in good breeding condition as well.

✔ **Feed egg food every day.**
Egg food is very nutritious and may prompt the birds to get into the breeding mood.

✔ **Make sure that the nest boxes are in a comfortable position for the pair — preferably high in a corner of the cage.**
The pair should feel very secure. The nest should be out of any bad weather, like rain, and be in a shady spot.

✔ **Remove aggressive birds from the cage or aviary if they're bothering the pair.**
Your pair will have trouble breeding when they're being hassled. They may not breed at all or may abandon eggs or babies. Also, another aggressive bird can kill one of the pair.

✔ **Offer a steady source of calcium, such as a cuttlebone.**
Breeding hens need extra calcium to aid in egg production. Calcium will leach from her bones if she doesn't have enough in her diet; this can cause tremendous health problems, including egg binding, and even death.

✔ **Offer a variety of nesting materials.**
Every finch pair is different in the materials they prefer. When they find the materials they like, they'll begin to line their nest.

✔ **Be sure they have clean, fresh drinking and bathing water.**
This is true for any bird, breeding or not. Water is another sign of "abundance," putting the pair at ease to breed.

✔ **Make sure that the pair is undisturbed.**
Too much noise or activity near the cage or nest can disrupt breeding or rearing of the babies.

✔ **Clean the nest between each *clutch* (group of eggs and/or babies).**
The nest will be soiled after each successful breeding.

Index

FOR DUMMIES®

Pet care essentials in plain English

DOG BREEDS

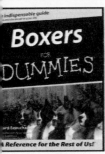

Boxers FOR DUMMIES

A Reference for the Rest of Us!

0-7645-5285-6

German Shepherds FOR DUMMIES

A Reference for the Rest of Us!

0-7645-5280-5

Golden Retrievers FOR DUMMIES

A Reference for the Rest of Us!

0-7645-5267-8

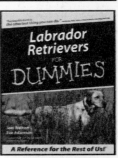

Labrador Retrievers FOR DUMMIES

A Reference for the Rest of Us!

0-7645-5281-3

Pugs FOR DUMMIES

Reference for the Rest of Us!

0-7645-54076-9

Retired Racing Greyhounds FOR DUMMIES

A Reference for the Rest of Us!

0-7645-5276-7

Siberian Huskies FOR DUMMIES

A Reference for the Rest of Us!

0-7645-5279-1

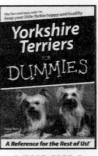

Yorkshire Terriers FOR DUMMIES

A Reference for the Rest of Us!

0-7645-6880-9

Also available:

Jack Russell Terriers For Dummies
(0-7645-5268-6)

Rottweilers For Dummies
(0-7645-5271-6)

Chihuahuas For Dummies
(0-7645-5284-8)

Dachshunds For Dummies
(0-7645-5289-9)

Pit Bulls For Dummies
(0-7645-5291-0)

DOG CARE, HEALTH, TRAINING, & BEHAVIOR

Puppies FOR DUMMIES

A Reference for the Rest of Us!

0-7645-5255-4

Dog Training FOR DUMMIES

A Reference for the Rest of Us!

0-7645-5286-4

Senior Dogs FOR DUMMIES

A Reference for the Rest of Us!

0-7645-5818-8

Also available:

Choosing a Dog For Dummies
(0-7645-5310-0)

Dog Health & Nutrition For Dummies
(0-7645-5318-6)

Dog Tricks For Dummies
(0-7645-5287-2)

House Training For Dummies
(0-7645-5349-6)

Dogs For Dummies, 2nd Edition
(0-7645-5274-0)

FOR DUMMIES

Pet care essentials in plain English

CATS & KITTENS

0-7645-5275-9

0-7645-4150-1

BIRDS

0-7645-5139-6

0-7645-5311-9

AMPHIBIANS & REPTILES

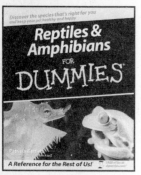

0-7645-2569-7

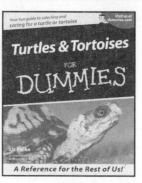

0-7645-5313-5

0-7645-5260-0

FISH & AQUARIUMS

0-7645-5156-6

0-7645-5340-2

SMALL ANIMALS

0-7645-5259-7

0-7645-0861-X